No More Perfect Kids offers wise counsel, genuine insight, and practical advice for parents, no matter how old your kids are. Mine are grown, and I still discovered many ways to improve my mothering skills. Savage and Koch are right: it's so important to love your kids "as is." Together they show us why, show us how, and show us what to do (and what not to do). A great read, a great guide.

— LIZ CURTIS HIGGS,
bestselling author of *The Girl's Still Got It*

No More Perfect Kids is one of those rare, must-read books that a parent will return to again and again. It is beautifully equipping and encouraging. Quite simply, incorporating these principles will be one of the most powerful, life-giving gifts you could ever give to your children.

— BRENNAN DEAN, president
Great Homeschool Conventions, Inc.

Wow. The message of Jill and Kathy's book can free every parent from those subtle, unrealistic expectations that we sometimes impose on ourselves and our kids. This easy-to-read and practical book gives us the hope and tools to achieve the ultimate prize: our child becoming the unique, irreplaceable individual God intends him or her to be. As a social researcher, I have talked to enough kids that I can unequivocally tell every parent, "Your child would love for you to read this book!"

— SHAUNTI FELDHAHN, social researcher, speaker, and
bestselling author of *For Women Only* and *For Parents Only*

For many Christians, the idea that everyone is made in God's image is just that: an idea. What does it look like to live as if this is really true? What does it look like to parent as if this is really true of our children? That's what this book is all about. In *No More Perfect Kids*, Jill Savage and Kathy Koch explain, illustrate, and illuminate what parenting image-bearers means. Even better, the book is full of incredibly practical things to do immediately. I'm a dad, and I really needed this book.

— JOHN STONESTREET, speaker and fellow for the Colson
Center for Christian Worldview and cohost of BreakPoint radio

No More Perfect Kids provides parents with a countercultural truth that needs to be understood and embraced. Our children are entrusted to us and we waste a lot of time doggedly pursuing "perfection" when we should be affirming God's unique design for our child. Jill Savage and Kathy Koch have created a much needed rallying cry parents are overdue to embrace: *No More Perfect Kids!*

— TRACEY EYSTER, founder and executive director of FamilyLife's
MomLife Today and author of *Be the Mom*

NO MORE PERFECT KIDS

Love Your Kids for Who They Are

JILL SAVAGE & KATHY KOCH, PhD

MOODY PUBLISHERS
CHICAGO

All Scripture quotations, unless otherwise indicated, are taken from the *Holy Bible, New International Version®*, NIV®. Copyright ©1973, 1978, 1984, 2011 by Biblica, Inc.™ Used by permission of Zondervan. All rights reserved worldwide. www.zondervan.com.

Scripture quotations marked NLT are taken from the *Holy Bible, New Living Translation*, copyright © 1996, 2004. Used by permission of Tyndale House Publishers, Inc., Wheaton, Illinois 60189, U.S.A. All rights reserved.

Scripture quotations marked THE MESSAGE are taken from *The Message*, copyright © by Eugene H. Peterson 1993, 1994, 1995. Used by permission of NavPress Publishing Group.

Scripture quotations marked NASB are taken from the *New American Standard Bible®*. Copyright © 1960, 1962, 1963, 1968, 1971, 1972, 1973, 1975, 1977, 1995 by The Lockman Foundation. Used by permission.

Scripture quotations marked AMP are taken from *The Amplified Bible*. Copyright © 1965, 1987 by The Zondervan Corporation. *The Amplified New Testament* copyright © 1958, 1987 by The Lockman Foundation. Used by permission.

Published in association with the literary agency of Transatlantic Agency.

Edited by Annette LaPlaca
Interior design: Smartt Guys design
Cover design: Faceout Studio
Cover images: iStock #8641435, #11352405, #19811578, #23247191, #25083410

Library of Congress Cataloging-in-Publication Data

Savage, Jill, 1964-
    No more perfect kids : love your kids for who they are / Jill Savage and Kathy Koch, PhD.
      pages cm
    Includes bibliographical references.
    ISBN 978-0-8024-1152-5
    1. Parent and child—Religious aspects. 2. Parenthood—Religious aspects. I. Koch, Kathy. II. Title.
    HQ755.85.S283 2014
    306.874—dc23

                                                    2013039487

We hope you enjoy this book from Moody Publishers. Our goal is to provide high-quality, thought-provoking books and products that connect truth to your real needs and challenges. For more information on other books and products written and produced from a biblical perspective, go to www.moodypublishers.com or write to:

Moody Publishers
820 N. LaSalle Boulevard
Chicago, IL 60610

3 5 7 9 10 8 6 4

Printed in the United States of America

We dedicate this book to our parents,
Duane and Patsy Fleener and
Don and Arlene Koch,
because they were always for us.
We're grateful they invested in us
and prioritized their role as parents.
We each became who God designed us
to be because of their love and support.

CONTENTS

Foreword

I once knew a young man who finished medical school and then decided that he did not want to be a medical doctor. He said, "I went to medical school to please my father. It was never really what I wanted to do. Now that my father has died, I want to pursue my own dreams." I have often wondered how many young men and women pursue their parents' dreams rather than their own.

As parents, all of us want to see our children succeed. However, our perceptions of success may not be in keeping with our child's abilities and interests. Not every young man is designed to be a fighter pilot or basketball player. Not every young lady is designed to be a doctor or a lawyer. However, each child is gifted to have a positive impact on

....

society. Our role as parents is to help our children discover and develop those abilities.

We don't always use the word *perfect*, but most parents do have a vision for what they want their child to become. That vision may include an image of the perfect child. But unless we are willing to release our perceptions of perfection, and place our children in the hands of a loving God who designed them for His own purposes, we may be greatly frustrated parents. On the other hand, when we seek to cooperate with God and help our children to unlock the innate abilities and develop physically, intellectually, emotionally, and spiritually, to become the person God designed them to become, we become successful parents.

No More Perfect Kids is designed to help you become a successful parent. Jill Savage and Dr. Kathy Koch bring to this subject their own unique perspectives and experiences. I think you will identify with the personal experiences of Jill, mother of five, as she reveals her own struggle in seeking to avoid perfection. I think you will also appreciate reading the statements of children and parents who have shared with Kathy at her seminars and presentations over the years. Kathy's expertise in how children learn, coupled with Jill's practical experience, make them a perfect team to write on the subject of child development.

I believe this book will help parents process their feelings of disappointment when their children are not developing physically, intellectually, emotionally, and spiritually as they had hoped. Conversely, it will give parents guidance in developing positive approaches to helping their children reach the unique potential that each child possesses.

When we give up the idea of being perfect parents and having

....

perfect children, we are far more likely to become *good* parents who produce *healthy* children. When this happens, you will have the deep satisfaction of knowing that you have cooperated with God in helping your children reach their God-given potential. Few things are more satisfying in life than the feeling of having succeeded as a parent.

GARY CHAPMAN, PhD

Author, *The 5 Love Languages of Children*

Introduction

When you were pregnant or in the process of adopting, what did you imagine your child would be like? Were you imagining a boy? Were you hoping it was a girl? Would she like sports? Would he play the piano? Whether you realize it or not, before your new family member made his arrival, you were already making a connection with your imagined child.

When your child finally arrived, the imagined child didn't go away. The real child made his appearance, and then you began to deal with the gap between the imagined child and the real child. This isn't a once-and-done challenge; it continues throughout childhood and the teen years as we come face-to-face with our real children, who are often nothing like our imagined children. Sometimes we even have trouble *knowing* our real children—because our hearts are still attached to the imagined children.

Every parent has secret hopes and dreams for his or her child. Sometimes we are aware of those dreams, and sometimes they are buried deep inside, rising to the surface only when the bubble of expectation is burst into a million pieces. The sooner we become aware of our expectations and align them with reality, the better it is for us and for our children. That's a big part of what we'll be helping you do on the pages of this book.

All children deserve to be celebrated for who they are. When we can identify the unique design of each of our children, resisting the urge to compare them to ourselves, their siblings, or other children, we set them free to be all they are created to be. Allowing our children the freedom to be their true selves is one of the best gifts we can give them. All children deserve to be celebrated for who they are.

When parents untangle themselves from their expectations, they free their children to be their best.

On the pages of this book, we'll explore something we call the Perfection Infection and how it affects our parenting. We'll look at the danger of unrealistic expectations and the security and peace found by children whose parents have realistic expectations. Then we will intersect our hopes and dreams with the core questions kids ask deep in their hearts: *Do you like me? Am I important to you? Is it okay that I'm unique? Who am I? Am I a failure? What's my purpose? Will you help me change?*

These questions are the same ones we once asked ourselves as children. The answers we concluded from our relationship with our own parents are still with us today. For some of us, our conclusions have served us well. We know we are loved, we don't need to please others, and we know both what we're good at and what we're not wired for at all! Others of us, however, still carry labels, a need to please people, and a sense of failure even into adulthood.

A child who has a parent who intentionally addresses these core questions of identity has a head start in this world. When parents untangle themselves from their expectations, they free their children to be their best. Our hope is to help you do just that!

To increase this book's practicality, we've included several appendixes. Parenting isn't about "hoping for the best." It's about being intentional in setting direction and teaching our kids what they need to know to function well in this world. Therefore, on the No More Perfect website (www.NoMorePerfect.com) you will find specific activities you can do with your kids to drive home the truths of this book.

This book is the first Hearts at Home book designed for both Mom and Dad to read. Don't dismay if your spouse isn't a reader—just share what you're learning along the way! However, if you both decide to read the book, we expect some great discussions will follow. There's a lot to think about when it comes to leading our children.

This book is coauthored, and we'd love to introduce you to each of us:

FROM JILL

Dr. Kathy Koch is one of the most beloved speakers at our Hearts at Home mom conferences. What I've seen is that when Dr. Kathy talks, moms listen! I've been that mom myself! In her work at Celebrate Kids, Inc., Dr. Kathy has dug deep into children's hearts to really understand what they need, what they struggle with, and how parents can help draw out who they are created to be. Dr. Kathy has devoted her lifework to help parents be the best they can be. Her workshops at Hearts at Home conferences are standing-room-only, with every mom in the room taking furious notes as Dr. Kathy shares her wonderful wisdom in her winsome way! Dr. Kathy lives in Texas, where she leads Celebrate Kids, Inc., a nonprofit organization dedicated to helping parents, educators, and children of all ages meet their core needs of security, identity, belonging, purpose, and competence in healthy ways. Dr. Kathy's contribution to this book is the core message of helping parents know and understand their unique children.

FROM DR. KATHY

I first encountered Jill at the 2011 Hearts at Home conference in Illinois, where she lives. I immediately resonated with her passion for moms and children and the ministry she began in 1994 to encourage, educate, and equip every mom in every season of motherhood. She values moms, has lived through the joys and pain of parenting with her husband, Mark, and is motherhood's perfect ambassador. Prioritizing her relationship with God, her husband, kids, and grandchildren, she has blessed thousands of moms with both her solid teaching and her vulnerable honesty. Better perhaps than anyone I know, she tells stories without glamorizing or diminishing pain while honoring those involved. Jill reminds us that relationships are hard work, but worth every tear. She models the benefits of putting one foot in front of the other and trusting that tomorrow is another day. Watching her, we know we can grow and God can honor the prayers and heart cry of His faithful

....

followers. Her illustrations and anecdotes bring my ideas to life. You'll be blessed by the suggestions she includes. I'm honored to partner with her and glad you're joining with us.

• • • •

For an easier read, we will write from one voice: Jill's. All pronouns will refer to Jill. Dr. Kathy will be identified in her illustrations and stories. The message of No More Perfect Kids is a blend of our shared passion to encourage parents and be a voice for the children.

Turn the page and dig deep with us. We're going to explore what goes on inside the head and the heart of a child and how we, as parents, can love our children for who they are and help them be all that God has created them to be!

CHAPTER 1

NO MORE *Perfect* KIDS

J stood outside the door of my six-month-old firstborn's room listening to her cry. She'd been changed. She'd been rocked. She'd been fed. Nothing calmed her. Finally, for my 3 a.m. sanity, I decided I just had to put her in her bed and let her fuss for a while. My best friend's son slept through the night after only two months. *Sweet little girl, why can't you sleep like my friend's little guy sleeps?* I was a new mom, and already my expectations for my first child were getting tangled up with comparisons and disappointments. I dreamed of cuddling my adored first baby, not of standing outside her bedroom door, exhausted, weeping along with her in frustration.

I found myself sitting on the sidelines of a soccer field—me, the sports-challenged momma—trying to figure out how to encourage my

. . . .

soccer-loving son. I'd much rather have been sitting next to him on a piano bench than sitting along the sidelines of a soccer game. *I'm trying to understand the game and be there to support you. Be patient with me, sweet boy.* My expectations were again rising to the surface: I dreamed of a piano-playing boy, not the sweaty, tousled teammate running up the soccer field.

I found myself trying to connect with my twelve-year-old daughter. This third child of mine likes fashion design. She loved to shop, not so much with the intention of buying but rather to see how clothes are designed and put together. I, on the other hand, hate to shop and don't have a "fashion design" bone in my body. I'd pay someone to shop for me if I could. *How did this fashion-challenged mom end up with a fashion-conscious daughter?* I never dreamed a fashionista could be born from a mom with a complete disinterest in style.

Child number four, who was in junior high, asked, "Mom, will you please help me study for a test?" Taking the study guide from his hands, I walked across the room to my recliner. When I turned around, I saw my thirteen-year-old son upside down in another recliner across the room. His head was in the seat and his feet were hanging over the back of the chair. I stopped myself from correcting him. He answered every study question correctly—upside down and all. *Lord, let me see my son through Your eyes. He's unique, one-of-a-kind, and much more than the ADHD label he carries.* I never dreamed I would have a child who struggled with ADD.

I found myself visiting our fifth child in his first of multiple hospitalizations for mental health issues. Ten years earlier, God had moved

We expected everything to be perfect.... Then we had kids.

heaven and earth to bring our son from an orphanage in Russia to our loving family in the middle of the cornfields of Illinois. He assimilated well in the early years after his adoption, but as he entered the late teen years, identity issues, attachment and personality disorders, depression, and more took up residence in our home. *This wasn't the life I pictured for you when we traveled across the ocean to bring you home.* I never dreamed our loving family could be touched by the heartbreak of mental illness.

Every parent does it. Before kids, we dreamed about what our family would look like. We thought about the way our family would interact with one another. We contemplated all the milestones our children would accomplish. We decided—in our mind—who our children would be. We imagined what they'd do. We anticipated what we would do together one-on-one and as a family. We expected everything to be perfect.

And then we had kids.

Parenting is harder than it looks. Even if our lives, our families, or our children are exactly like we imagined, challenges appear around every corner. Developmental stages are unfamiliar and at times, frustrating. We tell a child to "act your age," and then we realize he really is!

For some of us, our kids aren't quite like we imagined. Their temperament is a blend of both Dad and Mom, and we're not quite sure how to manage that. As they get older, we realize they don't have the interests we thought they would have or that we wanted them to have. Their talents are different from ours. They don't like the same things we like. They struggle in ways we don't understand. They don't make the decisions we'd make. Sometimes they don't make good decisions at all!

. . . .

Some of us may be dealing with even bigger disparities from our vision, like having a child with a medical condition, a mental or physical disability, or developmental delays. Those who are walking that journey are like people who thought they were going to live in Italy, but ended up in Holland instead. Still a pretty place, but very different from what they were expecting.

Most of us have expectations for each child. We expect him to grow and learn. We expect her to do her best. We expect him to behave and be responsible. We expect her to process life well. We expect him to act his age, but sometimes we forget—or just plain old don't know—what is actually normal behavior for a child his age! (And how realistic is this goal when we'd have to admit we don't always act our age?)

Let's face it: Life doesn't always look the way we imagined it would. We wanted a child, but we didn't realize it would mean sleepless nights for twelve months or more! We wanted to play catch in the backyard, but little Joey wants to play piano in the living room instead. We longed to have a child who loved to learn, only to find ourselves in parent-teacher conferences trying to figure out why Susie is barely passing her classes. We anticipated laughter and love and overlooked the fact that tears, tantrums, and tough stuff would also be a part of the package. We love our children with all of our hearts, but we don't always know what to do when our expectations don't match reality. What do we do when our expectations don't match reality?

Over time, thoughts like these may cross our minds: *I wish she were more like her brother*, or, *I never thought I'd have a kid who wants to stay home and read after school instead of getting involved in extracurricular activities*, or, *I wish my toddler would get on a regular nap schedule.*

. . . .

When we are disappointed, frustrated, confused, or even disillusioned, these thoughts are natural ones. However, when we spend too much time thinking or wishing that someone should be different, we can become frustrated and discouraged at the least, and critical, nagging, and even rejecting at the worst.

At some point, every parent comes face-to-face with putting fantasy aside and embracing reality. *This is the real child. These are the real circumstances of my life. These are uncharted waters for me to navigate. How do I guide and lead a child I sometimes don't understand? How do I love the infant, child, teenager, or young adult I have right here in front of me and not wish she was any different? How can I delight in how he is created even though it's different from what I imagined? How do I inspire and encourage but not expect perfection from my child? How do I celebrate progress and stay clear of unrealistic expectations?*

These are the questions we will answer on the coming pages. Our children are unique gifts from God who deserve to be celebrated. They have been designed by their Creator to contribute to this world in unique ways. They have present value and potential just waiting to be released. The key for us is to see that potential in them on the good days and on the bad days, as well. Let's launch a journey of discovery to embrace who our children really are and to celebrate how they are uniquely designed!

WHERE DOES IT BEGIN?

Upon entering the room, you're surprised your child is standing. You realize a big milestone is about to occur.

You don't shout, "Sit down. You might hurt yourself!" Instead, you

. . . .

have someone run to get the video camera while you get in position. You expect progress, and you show that to your child through your behavior and language.

Positioning yourself four feet away with your arms outstretched, you smile broadly and use only an encouraging tone of voice. Focused on the goal, you communicate, "Come to Momma!"

We're looking for progress, not perfection.

One step. Then another. A fall. A second try will appear as a false start. Over the next few days there are missteps. Attempts. Half-steps. Fall downs.

There aren't "mistakes," though. We would never tell people our child made a mistake trying to walk, even if he fell down on his tenth attempt. Rather, it is more likely we would announce his every attempt. We call our parents, siblings, and friends and perhaps even post it on Facebook: "Jared tried to walk today!" This is our attitude because we're looking for progress, not perfection—for growth, not completion.

We know error-free walking is the goal. It's possible, but only if it's the destination. Perfection can't be the journey. The journey must be built on faith in the possibilities and an expectation for good, better, and then best.

As you've probably noticed, children don't crawl for long. They pull themselves up, walk around things, walk alone, skip, gallop, and eventually run. When they fall down doing any of those things, they almost always pick themselves up and keep going unless we react as if they should be upset. Gasping, looking at them with alarm, running toward them, and asking if they're okay will likely cause the tears to flow even if they are not hurt by the stumble. Our reactions are often mirrored by our children's.

Their goal to walk is accomplished and celebrated. Maybe you expected to reach "your goal." But walking is their goal, too. That's another reason children don't crawl. At a young age, they long for progress. When I watch my ten-month-old granddaughter pulling herself up and walking around furniture, I realize she's not that much different from my teenage sons still at home who look for progress in the form of independence.

What if, throughout their growing-up years, we had a "Come to Momma!" perspective? What difference would it make if we could see progress even in the smallest of ways from our preschooler, grade-schooler, our teenager, our young adult? What if we expected them to stumble along the way and we didn't consider that stumble a mistake? What if we stayed at four feet away, not eight? What if our arms are reached toward our children, not folded in front of us? What if we smiled instead of frowned? What if we had an encouraging, optimistic tone in our voices, issuing a request our children want to fulfill, not demands they can't live up to?

What if our children had a "Come to Momma!" belief system? *I can accomplish what my parents are asking me to do. Attempts aren't failure; they are part of life. I can pick myself up to try again. Perfection may never be reached or even necessary because I know my parents will celebrate my progress.*

If we want this to happen, it might require us to make some changes in how we think and how we respond. This kind of motivating affirmation might not be something we experienced ourselves when we were

. . . .

children, so we'll have to learn something new and celebrate our own progress along the way. As parents, we hold an incredible power over how our children feel about themselves and their relationship with us.

THE POWER OF EXPECTATIONS

We know too much of a good thing is not a good thing: too much ice cream, too much laundry, too many phone calls, too many leaves to rake—and expectations that are too high.

Most of us begin parenting with high expectations for our children because we love them and want the best for them. If our children meet those, we set new ones that are more challenging. After all, they've proven they're capable and we don't want them to stop growing or learning. It's all very innocent—at the beginning.

What if our arms are reached toward our children, not folded in front of us?

However, this can start the mountain climb. If we're always setting higher and higher expectations, our children can get the idea we're never satisfied. Just when they achieve something, and they think we'll be happy and they can relax, we announce something else we expect them to do. When we don't acknowledge they have met our expectations, they easily assume we're not satisfied.

When asking children of any age why they think their parents expect perfection, answers come easily. Responses sound something like this: "They told me I needed to improve. I agreed I could do better. I did. I got a better grade. They didn't say 'good job' or 'thank you.' They just said, 'You can do better!'"

In her research at Celebrate Kids, Dr. Kathy indicates that some kids comment further. Some conclude simply, "I can never please my parents." That's a dangerous conclusion for kids to reach because they just might stop trying. They may no longer care what we want them to do. They may not believe us when we say, "We just want you to do your best." Some tell us they purposefully don't improve because of the pressure that follows. This is common in both academics and athletics. Other kids tell us they're angry because they feel misled. One high school boy proclaimed to Dr. Kathy, "If my dad wanted a perfect score, I wish he would have just told me that."

When our children do less than a great job on something, we don't want a pattern of sloppy work or mistakes to take root so we indicate we're concerned, unhappy, or disappointed. But, depending on how we respond to their work, children can misinterpret our concerns. They may believe we can never be satisfied and that perfection is what we want. They may not be able to separate their work from themselves, thinking they are their work. *If Daddy doesn't like my work, he doesn't like me.*

Setting appropriate and fair expectations is a key to successful parenting. This requires us to know our children—really know our kids. If our goals are too low, children won't achieve as much as they might have. If they're too high, children may get frustrated and give up. In either case, they may not achieve what they're capable of. Setting appropriate expectations requires us to *really* know our children.

Just like Goldilocks looked for a chair, porridge, and a bed that were "just right," parents need to look for expectations that are "just right" for each child. Like Goldilocks, we need to try them out. How does our oldest respond to this expectation? How does our youngest respond

....

to this one? How can I best explain this so he'll understand? Through perceptive, close observations during trial-by-error efforts, we should be able to land on expectations that are "just right." Not too easy and not too hard. Challenging without being frustrating. Achievable with effort. Personalized. Not a one-size-fits-all approach.

What's healthier than expecting perfection? It's certainly not expecting numerous errors and failure. Rather, it's expecting children to fully use their abilities and attitudes to be who they were designed to be. We want them to fully come into their own.

We risk great damage to children when we expect them to be who they weren't created to be. Expecting them to give us what they can't doesn't work. Perhaps you've read the clever story that makes this point using animals. For example, rabbits are good at hopping. If we tried to teach them to fly and even graded them on their ability, they'd flunk. And, using all their energy to try to learn to fly may cause the rabbits to dismiss and no longer value or use their hopping ability. Hopping may no longer bring them joy.

If a child is a musical genius capable of quickly memorizing and beautifully playing complex piano pieces, that's what she should do. Choosing easier music or being satisfied with less than stellar performances would not be right. She wouldn't be honoring her Creator because she'd be dismissing the way she was made.

But expecting this same girl to consistently earn perfect grades in math classes may be unfair. It's not right to assume that because she can do one thing well (memorize music), she should be able to do another thing well (memorize math facts). Rather, we must look for and use evidence when setting goals and expectations for our children. When children see us dismiss evidence that things are easy or hard, they're discouraged.

One sixth-grader bounded out the door, happy finally to be attending middle school. However, his joy was immediately sucked out of him when he heard his dad proclaim as he was leaving, "You're going to have a great year in math." Later that day, this boy angrily questioned Dr. Kathy, "I don't know what my dad thinks happened over the summer to make me smart all of a sudden in math. But nothing happened. Can't he just accept the fact that math is hard for me?"

THE POWER OF THE GREENER-GRASS SYNDROME

Setting unrealistic expectations or constantly raising them is not the only thing we do to cause our children to infer that we want them to be perfect. If we're never satisfied with ourselves and they hear us constantly complaining and comparing, they can get the wrong idea. What have they recently heard *you* say?

"Our kitchen is way too small. I can't live like this!"

"This traffic is horrible! I should have gone a different way."

"Look at all those weeds. Our lawn is the worst on the block."

No wonder kids get the idea we're hard to please and nothing is ever good enough. With parenting, much is caught. We need to ask ourselves, "What are my kids 'catching' from me?"

Never being satisfied makes for a horrible existence. It's hard enough for adults who may have developed a thick skin and some coping mechanisms. However, it's very damaging to children. They'll never experience the joy and peace associated with contentment. Instead, they'll find themselves

Trying, never succeeding.

Hoping, always disappointed.

Eventually stopping, no longer risking.

Always comparing.

Critique hurts too much. Perfectionists tend to see even minor imperfections. That's bad enough, but they usually take it one step further. They decide these imperfections make themselves and others totally unacceptable. This can hurt their ability to have healthy relationships. Perfectionists tend to think imperfections are totally unacceptable.

Contentment isn't easy. Maybe it's never been, but today it's made extra challenging by how easy it is to compare. We can always find someone smarter, better, prettier, or more organized. With television commercials constantly reminding us of what we do not own, magazine covers blaring the perfect look, and Pinterest and Facebook updates, pictures, and videos giving even strong adults inferiority complexes, no wonder it's hard to be content. We can quickly begin to feel bad about ourselves.

Watch out for the syndrome, though. You know it: It robs you of joy, peace, and satisfaction. It replaces contentment with questions, doubt, and confusion. You can identify it by evaluating your thought life. Do you find yourself thinking:

If I had her kitchen, I'd cook better meals and could entertain.

I wish we lived where there wasn't any traffic. Then I'd take the kids lots of fun places.

....

I cannot believe how bad our lawn looks compared to the corner property. I can't even do that right!

I wish we had a nicer car. Our old car looks so bad compared to our neighbor's car.

If we had more money, we could do _____.

It's the Greener-Grass Syndrome. When we believe the grass is always greener on the other side of the fence, we're quickly dissatisfied. We're critical. We can become angry.

The Syndrome causes us to think:

I'd be happy if . . .

If my kids were better readers, then . . .

Our kids would be better behaved if . . .

Contentment involves confidently living life *as it is*. We parent our kids *as they are*. When we embrace our real lives and our real kids and our real spouses, we won't doubt everything. We won't blame things on others. We won't ask lots of What-if questions. We won't constantly second-guess ourselves. We won't live with the "If only . . ." wondering mindset.

When we're able to be content with what is, we won't assume "this" or "that" would make us happier. We won't waste much time thinking we should have bought a different house, married someone else, or stopped after two children. We won't waste time being angry about a lost opportunity. We won't obsess on a negative comment on our work review. We won't cry over spilt milk or miss the silver lining because we're only looking for gold.

Contentment means we won't focus on what we don't have, what we can't do, and what's wrong with everything and everyone around us.

. . . .

We'll be aware of these things, because we know life can't be perfect, but we won't focus there. Rather, we'll focus on what we *do* have, what we *can do*, and what's right with the world—including our part of the world.

Contentment and perfectionism can't exist together. Contentment says we're satisfied. Perfectionism says we never are.

Our contentment is tied to having realistic expectations about ourselves. This is only possible when we know ourselves well. We must be honest and know if there are strengths we haven't yet tapped into and weaknesses we consider permanent and damaging. We can compare ourselves against our former selves rather than to an inaccurate view of who we are or who we wish we were. We resist the urge to determine if we're okay or not based on comparisons to someone else.

Contentment is not the same as stagnating at a plateau.

We must value our abilities without developing pride and accept our weaknesses without letting them defeat us. Content people are comfortable in their own skin. We have learned to ignore signs in the culture and words from "friends" who say we should have much more than we have or could be much more than what we are. Content parents don't constantly compare themselves to others. They're more grateful for what they have than concerned about what they don't have.

Adults who are content with themselves will want their children to be content. They've learned it's not the same as stagnating at a plateau or being satisfied with mediocrity or with less than their potential capability. Too often guilt and shame can be connected to those decisions. Parents who are content in themselves have learned to value peace and want their children to experience that. They like the calm that accompanies contentment and long for their children to know that well.

. . . .

They also appreciate contentment's joy and other-centeredness, and they want their kids to experience these qualities.

Contentment doesn't make parents or their children settle for less. The opposite is true! Contentment actually allows us to risk more. We strive to learn something new. We may more willingly try for a promotion because our lives don't depend on getting it. We'll have people over for dinner even if the house isn't perfect. We may even serve company a new recipe we haven't fed our family first.

Children who are content and haven't been taught the What-if? thinking pattern of the Greener-Grass Syndrome will more likely become who God intended for them to be. They'll be comfortable in their own skin and learn to be satisfied with their personal strengths, talents, and interests. They'll use them, develop them, and serve God with them. Their weaknesses won't scare them, define them, or control them.

Isn't that what you and I want for our kids? We want them to be free to be themselves in a world that screams for conformity. We long to be their cheerleaders in spite of their mistakes. We want them to be the best they can be. We want them to be themselves—not perfect, just all they can be.

How do we get there? How can we steer clear of expecting perfection? How can we see our kids through the eyes of our Creator? Keep reading! There are important questions to be asked and important lessons for us, as parents, to learn.

· · · · · · · ·

Cheri's Story

It was a complete meltdown. I had asked one simple question. She flung her little five-year-old body onto the floor. I was instantly irritated. My voice kept rising higher while trying to remain calm. My first instinct was, *Are you kidding me?!* My second instinct was that I needed to get this kid to bed. Quickly, my question turned into a demand.

After three kids, countless tantrums, and thirteen years of motherhood, why do I still let these meltdowns get to me?

Perfection.

It's an ugly word.

I expect too much from my kids. I ignore the cues. I knew my little girl had been outside swimming, pretending, eating, and laughing all day long with the neighbor kids. I knew she had only recently recovered from an ear infection and sore throat. I knew she had not been sleeping well. I knew she was exhausted. Under all these circumstances, I still expected her to cooperate, without argument.

Once I realized what I was doing, I backed off my demand. We cuddled. She stopped crying, and a compromise was reached. We began again. I'm not a perfect mom. I don't have perfect kids. We get by with grace and forgiveness and lessons learned.

Don't be too hard on your kids. Pay attention to their cues. Forgive. Love.[1]

CHAPTER 2

THE *Perfection* INFECTION
COLLIDES WITH PARENTING

*T*he clouds were hanging low, the breeze was brisk, and the waves were strong enough that diehard surfers entered the ocean. After they walked out a good way, they waited to catch the perfect wave. There's nothing wrong with surfers seeking a perfect ride. Waiting for the perfect child, on the other hand, isn't quite the same. Children won't be perfect. They're imperfect. They're children, so they'll make mistakes—that's actually how they learn and make progress.

Children rarely choose to strive for perfection on their own. Rather, their parents' expectations and reactions to their mistakes convince them they have no choice. As parents, we hold some power over how our kids think and feel about themselves. Don't be afraid of that power

....

though. When you and I understand it and embrace it, we take steps in the right direction to successfully keep perfection out of our parenting.

THE PERFECTION INFECTION AT HOME

In my book *No More Perfect Moms*, I introduced the concept of the Perfection Infection—the effect on our minds and spirits of the widespread, sanitized, airbrushed standards we see every day in the world around us and our deplorable tendency to compare ourselves.

The media saturation of our society contributes to the Perfection Infection:

> In the checkout aisle at Wal-Mart . . . [we] see pictures of "perfect" houses, "perfect" bodies, and "perfect" families splashed on the front of the magazines we walk by to pay for our groceries. . . . The photos are airbrushed, the stories are edited, and the guarantee of perfection is overpromised in order to sell magazines.
>
> While magazines give us unrealistic visual images to compare our real bodies and our real homes to, we can thank Hollywood for painting unrealistic relational pictures for us. Every sitcom presents and resolves some kind of problem in a thirty-minute time span. Every movie presents some event or season of life that gets tidily wrapped up within a mere two hours . . . Even the reality shows aren't real. They have been cut and edited so much that they sometimes misrepresent what really happened in a scene.[2]

In our socially connected generation, we know and keep up with a vast number of friends and acquaintances, so we have numerous people with whom we can compare our reality with our perceived view of their reality! If you spend some time with Facebook, Twitter, or Pinterest, you'll know how easily comparison comes into play:

> As we look at the status someone posts, we think, "I wish my kid would say something cute like that." Or "I wish I could say something nice like that about my husband." On Pinterest, we can find ourselves wishing we had more creativity or better ideas as we look at all the great organizational tools or craft projects people share.[3]

All this comparison is forcefully tied to our expectations. The more we compare, the higher our expectations climb. There it is: the Perfection Infection. We didn't realize we'd started expecting our problems to be solved in thirty minutes (or maybe two hours), TV or movie style. We didn't realize we'd started expecting burnished, flawless skin like the supermodel in the magazine ad or on the commercial. We respond with unconscious, instinctive longing to magazine spreads depicting beautiful kitchens and family rooms with vases of flowers for accents and no toys on the floor or unopened mail on the countertops. "Our expectations are fueled by a constant barrage of 'perfect' scenes and images we see in our media-saturated society."[4]

Without realizing it, we have become inundated with perfection. It's the subtlest infiltration! With near-perfection hitting our eyes at every turn, it's no wonder our desires begin to be shaped with expectations of a perfect house, a perfect body, a perfect husband, a perfect wife—and perfect kids. Like weather and water can erode a bluff or beach over time, our real-life satisfaction—that is, satisfaction with our real homes, our real bodies, our real spouses, and our real kids—is being eroded. "If we don't recognize it, the discontentment can turn

....

into disappointment, and then the disappointment can eventually turn into disillusionment. However, the disillusionment cannot really be resolved because what you are looking for—the perfect house, the perfect job, the perfect child—simply does not exist."[5]

Without effort, the Perfection Infection slips unnoticed right into our parenting expectations. When it does, we move into dangerous territory that not only hurts our relationship with our child, but it also can affect how our children see the world and themselves.

THE TEN DANGERS OF PERFECTION INFECTION PARENTING

There are many negative consequences of perfectionism. Maybe you can agree with that because you were raised in an environment of off-the-charts expectations to which you could never measure up. You don't want to create that same environment for your kids, but you honestly don't know how to effectively parent any other way.

Maybe you've seen other parents putting too high of expectations on their kids. One mom cringed as she watched a father tell his son he could do better after he had won a swim meet but hadn't improved his time. All the dad could see was that his personal goal for his son to improve his time hadn't been accomplished. The dad couldn't see that the son had swum well and even won his race!

Maybe you've caught yourself expecting too much. Just because somebody else's two-year-old is potty-trained doesn't mean your two-year-old is ready for potty-training. Your expectations could be set from previous parenting experience such as subconsciously comparing your strong-willed third child to your first two easy-to-raise children.

· · · · · · · ·

Regardless of our experiences with high-expectation, perfectionist parenting, it is important for us to understand the power we have as parents to influence the way our kids see themselves and the world around them. Because of this power, we should be motivated to examine ourselves and our relationships with our children.

Do they *think* we expect them to be perfect? It doesn't matter what we *say* we want. What matters is what *they* pick up on because of our parenting style.

In an effort to fully understand the power of expecting perfection, let's examine the ten dangers of perfectionism. See if you can read these in two ways: 1) through your own childhood experience, and 2) through the eyes of your children.

Danger #1: Children won't ask for help because they can't admit they need it.

This can be relatively harmless if they just need help with a homework question, but harmful if they can't ask how to handle a bully or handle a dating issue. We want our kids to feel safe to ask about anything. People who feel comfortable asking questions are people who know it's okay not to know something. They understand that "not knowing" is normal. When kids are afraid to ask questions, they are usually feeling that it's not okay to not know something and *perfect people never need help.*

Ask yourself: As a child, was I afraid to ask my parents for help?

Ask yourself: As a parent, do I see my child being afraid to ask me for help?

Danger #2: Children will resist trying new things.

When children are forced to try something new, they will be stressed because it's hard to be perfect when a task is brand-new. Therefore, they'll learn less and experience less of life. They'll plateau and not reach their potential. Kids who are adventurous and willing to try new things aren't afraid of failing. They know they've got to start somewhere and that the first time is just that—the first time! When kids are afraid to try new things, they are often internally thinking that *perfect people never make mistakes*. Kids may fear to try new things if they think perfect people never make mistakes.

Ask yourself: As a child, was I afraid of trying new things?

Ask yourself: As a parent, do I see my child being afraid to try new things?

Danger #3: Children who don't make mistakes won't develop resiliency.

The art of bouncing back and recovering strength quickly is important. Because they try to avoid mistakes at all costs, when these children do make mistakes, they may be crushed. A type of emotional paralysis will prevent them from making new attempts. They'll more likely believe mistakes are horrible things that must be avoided so they want to stay as far away from the failing experience as possible. Failure is perceived to be a far worse experience than it really is. These kids tell themselves, "Mistakes are terrible!"

Ask yourself: As a child, was I resilient and unafraid of making mistakes?

Ask yourself: As a parent, do I see my child being resilient and un-afraid of making mistakes?

Danger #4: Children will relate to parents from a perspective of fear.

These children won't want to make mistakes in front of their parents, and they won't want their parents to find out about errors they already made. They may try to hide and may wish they were invisible. They won't want to disappoint their parents and hear critical comments that are far too often a part of this parenting style. They think, *My parents will be mad if they find out I made another mistake.*

Ask yourself: As a child, was I afraid of my parents finding out I messed up?

Ask yourself: As a parent, do I see my child being afraid of me or of me finding out something?

Danger #5: Children may develop a negative and critical perspective toward themselves and others.

Because perfectionist parents are often negative and critical, children pick up the family culture. This negativity will affect their relation-ships with family, peers, and authorities. It will also skew how they see themselves and perceive their abilities. Instead of seeing the good, they focus on the bad. *I can't do anything right, but neither can anyone else. At least I'm not the only one messing up.*

Ask yourself: As a child, did I feel criticized by my parents?

Ask yourself: As a parent, does my child hear more negative than positive from me?

• • • • • • • •

Danger #6: Children may expect perfectionism from others even though they don't like trying to meet the expectation themselves.

Because of the expectation of perfection, people will regularly disappoint these children. People won't be free to be themselves. When everyone is guarded and tentative because mistakes could be made or discovered, relationships aren't deep and real. The lack of authenticity and honesty results in either superficial relationships or broken relationships. Healthy friendships are unlikely. Expectations of perfection prevent the authenticity and honesty that lead to healthy relationships.

Growing up, I didn't have a lot of friendships and often found myself disappointed by the friends I did have. Looking back, I now realize that some of that stemmed from my high expectations of myself and others. I often thought, *Why don't I have any real friends I can just have fun with?*

> *Ask yourself: Growing up, did I struggle with friendships or high expectations of others?*

> *Ask yourself: As a parent, do I see my child having unrealistic expectations of others?*

Danger #7: Children will focus primarily on what they cannot do, rather than what they can do.

Because parents who desire perfection point out what children do wrong rather than noticing or acknowledging what they do right, their children will primarily be familiar with what they cannot do.

Knowing weaknesses and challenges without knowing strengths is not a good combination. It's likely the children's weaknesses will win, and the children will be less productive and will lead a life without

....

purpose. For example, spelling doesn't come easily to Kathy, but she is word-smart. When writing, this allows her to choose synonyms she can spell. She has learned how to use a thesaurus rather than a dictionary. For example, she can look up "extraordinary" to find "phenomenal." She also uses a Miss-spellers Dictionary and uses the auto-correct feature in Microsoft Word more than others might. Without being affirmed through the years for her ideas and her ability to use words well, Kathy may have decided she couldn't write because spelling wasn't easy. Her good gift would have gone undeveloped because of a focus on her weakness.

Unlike Kathy, children raised with a heightened awareness of weaknesses—without awareness of strengths they can use to compensate for those problems and to improve themselves—won't be able to do much of anything. They'll doubt they can make progress. They may view weaknesses as permanent conditions, which will further decrease hope. They'll think, *My parents can always find something I do wrong. I can't do anything right and I'll never improve.* Focusing on weaknesses and challenges can make children lose hope in their own progress.

Ask yourself: As a child, was I more in tune with my strengths or weaknesses?

Ask yourself: As a parent, do I see my children focusing more on their strengths or their weaknesses? Which are they more in tune with?

Danger # 8: Children expected to be perfect may hesitate to own and believe in their successes because of the stress.

....

43

Some children make mistakes on purpose because not being perfect is less stressful than achieving the ultimate goal parents have put before them. They know the bar will be raised for an even better performance tomorrow. Once parents find out what children are capable of, they don't like accepting less. This adds to the pressure children experience. A young boy looked right at Kathy once when they were talking about his misbehavior. He confidently stated, "Oh, I know how to make my bed and I could make it, but I won't." When Kathy asked why, he responded, "Once my mom knows I can make it, she'll yell even more when I don't. At least now she's not sure." Sometimes children think, *I could do more, but I can't afford for my parents to find out. Mostly they're unhappy now. I don't want them mad, too.*

> *Ask yourself: Did you underperform as a child or teenager in an effort to keep stress at bay?*
>
> *Ask yourself: As a parent, might my kids be underperforming to keep me off their backs?*

Danger #9: Children will not believe in or experience the beauty of unconditional love.

Children of perfectionist parents may try to earn their parents' love, attention, and acceptance by being good enough and/or doing things well enough—even perfectly. They may feel like they always have to perform well to keep their parents happy.

One teenager told me, "I wish I felt like my parents loved me all the time. I just feel like they love me when I do things the way they want me to."

When expectations are too high, children may think, *My parents don't love me. They just love what I do when I do it perfectly.*

Ask yourself: As a child, did I feel unconditional love from my parents?

Ask yourself: As a parent, do I exhibit unconditional love to my children?

Danger #10: Being raised with perfection as a goal can negatively influence children's spiritual growth and how they relate to the God of the Bible.

Since they've learned to not ask their parents for help, children may not ask God for help either. Because they've learned to hide their struggles and mistakes from their parents, they may run *from* God when they sin. They may never fully experience His grace and unconditional love. They will try to earn His love and respect like they've tried to do with their parents. Additionally, if they believe they actually can be perfect, they may decide they don't need Jesus at all. They might actually come to think, *I can save myself. I don't need this Jesus they talk about.*

Ask yourself: Growing up, was I afraid of God?

Ask yourself: As a parent, do my children know and respond well to God's love and grace?

When I considered each of these questions, I got some mixed answers. I definitely carried some perfectionistic tendencies into my parenting, but I'm not convinced they all came from the way I was parented. Some of them seem to be intrinsic for me as part of my temperament and personality. That may be true for some of your kids, too. At the same time,

. . . .

45

I can also see how my parents' natural affirmation of achievement fed into my natural tendency to pursue perfection. As parents we need to know our children. We need to be perceptive, observant, and watchful. Do you already have a high achiever? When you affirm *effort* as much as *accomplishment,* your influence can be used to bring balance to their perfectionistic tendencies.

As you read about the ten dangers, did you find your child exhibiting some of the described behaviors? Maybe you didn't realize that the Perfection Infection had already reached that child. Do you have some insight into better understanding what might be going on in his head? More than anything, you can be more perceptive today than you were yesterday. And change is possible!

WHAT'S THE DIFFERENCE BETWEEN PERFECTION AND EXCELLENCE?

In order to fully understand the Perfection Infection in our own lives and in our parenting, it's important for us to understand the difference between excellence and perfection. We want to do our best and we want our kids to do their best, but when does excellence cross over into perfection? Some short answers are:

Excellence is something done well. Perfection is something done without fault.

Excellence is attainable. Perfection is unattainable.

Excellence is positive. Perfection is negative.

Excellence is satisfying. Perfection is never satisfied.

Excellence is freeing. Perfection is binding.

Excellence allows for failure. Perfection punishes failure.

. . . .

Excellence expects mistakes. Perfection panics at mistakes.

Excellence is growing. Perfection is dying.

Excellence is learning. Perfection is performing.

Excellence is open. Perfection is closed.

Excellence is motivated by confidence. Perfection is motivated by fear.

Excellence comes from God. Expectation of perfection comes from the world.

What does choosing excellence over perfectionism look like in the real world? Here's an example: A mom is supposed to provide snacks for her son's baseball team. Her desire is to make something homemade. However, she's had two sick children, a husband who's been putting in overtime, and her parents who live nearby have needed more help than usual. This week, baking is not something that can be realistically accomplished. In freedom, she picks up cupcakes at the bakery of her grocery store. This is an excellent choice based upon her limitations and what is going on in her life. This choice carries no sense of failure. She accomplished what she needed to accomplish in the best way for her family.

Excellence allows for many ways to accomplish something. It allows for context. Perfection says there is only one way to accomplish something. There is no context or consideration made.

Perfection steals our joy and results in hopelessness. It sets us up for failure. If we expect perfection from ourselves, we will be in perpetual disappointment. If we expect perfection from others, we will become hypercritical.

Excellence motivates us to do well within the reality of our temperaments, our talents, and our circumstances. We "hit the mark" in the context of all those things. When we expect excellence from ourselves, we work toward a goal cushioned with grace. When we expect excellence from others, we set goals and encourage them under the umbrella of grace, which allows for humanity—mistakes and all.

We are motivated to excellence out of our relationship with a loving, grace-filled God who is perfecting—or improving—us every day. We are encouraged in Colossians 3:23 with these words: *"Work willingly at whatever you do, as though you were working for the Lord rather than for people"* (NLT). Excellence happens when we give our best to God, knowing that our best can't be perfect because perfection can't happen here on earth. Excellence happens when we give our best to God, knowing that it won't be perfect.

Excellence is empowering. Perfection is rejecting. I want to be an empowering wife, mother, daughter, sister, and friend. That's why resisting perfection is so important. I want to embrace *what is* in my kids rather than lament *what isn't*. I want to see possibilities, not liabilities in each child God has given me.

When I look at the world, and especially at my kids, through the lens of the Perfection Infection, my perspective is skewed and I'm not able to see things as they really are. The Perfection Infection keeps my expectations of myself and of others unrealistic. When I compare my "imagined child" to my real child, the Perfection Infection widens the gap and keeps me from really knowing my child and celebrating who he is.

However, there's no need to feel guilt or shame for yesterday. We are writing to give you hope for tomorrow. There is a way to eradicate the Perfection Infection from our parenting. Before we jump into the core questions kids ask in their hearts and how to practically embrace our perfectly imperfect kids, we want to look at the cure for the Perfection Infection in our parenting. The prognosis is good if we will simply apply the antidotes to our own hearts first.

THE CURE FOR THE PERFECTION INFECTION IN PARENTING

Anna Quindlen once wrote, "The thing that is really hard, and really amazing, is giving up on being perfect and beginning the work of becoming yourself." She's reaching for the cure! When we recognize the Perfection Infection in our own lives, resist the urge to compare ourselves to others, and embrace who we really are, we experience an incredible freedom and contentment.

In *No More Perfect Moms*, I introduced the antidotes of humility, confidence, courage, and grace that help us eradicate the Perfection Infection in our own lives. When it comes to our parenting, I believe similar antidotes exist. These antidotes help us keep the Perfection Infection out of our parenting, help us resist the urge to compare our kids to others, and help us embrace who our kids really are. When applied liberally, these antidotes help create a home environment that gives our kids the freedom to fully be themselves. They experience contentment and a sense of safety and security when their parents allow them to be wholly who God created them to be.

The antidotes for the Perfection Infection in parenting are compassion, perception, acceptance, and love. Let's explore each of these for a moment.

. . . .

49

Compassion

In my past parenting life—before I got serious about addressing the Perfection Infection in my own parenting—I was a "buck up" mom. *Push through the pain. You're okay. Don't dwell on the disappointment; instead look to the future.* However, God's been softening my heart on this. Sometimes I need to just listen to my kids. I need to feel their pain without a need to fix it.

Words like *empathy* and *compassion* haven't always been on the short list of my character traits. Don't get me wrong: If my little one fell and scraped a knee, I was quick to scoop him up and head to my favorite rocking chair until the tears stopped. I've always been good about taking care of physical pain. It's the emotional pain I haven't always been good about tending to. If I'm honest, I'll acknowledge that I haven't always known how to tend to my own emotional pain.

Learning to listen with empathy builds trust and intimacy with your kids.

That's hard to admit, but true. From listening to and encouraging parents for twenty-plus years, I know I'm not alone. Dealing with emotional pain is hard for many of us. Most of us didn't see it modeled well in our families of origin. Quite frankly, even now it's not comfortable for most of us to tune into our feelings and be vulnerable. We lack self-compassion, which is the first step to showing compassion to those we love.

In an effort to learn to listen better and "feel" right along with my loved ones, I'm finding statements like these are helpful:

"I bet that was so disappointing."

"I'm sure that hurt your heart deeply."

"That breaks my heart. I would imagine it broke yours."

. . . .

"I'm so sorry. I'm sure that was painful for you to experience."

I'm discovering that learning to listen with empathy is building trust and intimacy with my kids. It's causing others to feel validated and loved. It's also helping me to slow down, tune in, and really connect to those I love.

Author and speaker Tammy Maltby shared with me, "Compassion is a choice. We must choose to see. We must choose to reach out to the other person and weep when they weep. We use our tears and pain to relate, to build a bridge into another person's reality. It is one of God's most powerful tools."

Feel or fix? Compassion feels. It builds bridges. The next time your daughter has a bad day, try the "feel" approach with her. Resist the urge to "fix." When your son tells you a story about something that happened to him, intentionally put yourself in his shoes and "feel" his pain or his excitement. By doing so, you'll apply the antidote of compassion that will allow you to create a sense of safety and security in your home and in the relationships that mean the most to you.

Perception

As a parent, you know it's important to be in tune with your kids. What do they like? What do they dislike? Do they need alone time? Are they creative? Athletic? Musical? What is important to them?

I'll admit that, with five children, there have been times when I've simply parented "the herd." I've seen them as a group rather than the individuals that they are. The more perceptive I've become, the more I am able to see them as unique human beings who have different personalities, temperaments, and skills.

....

Perception not only helps us see how a child is wired, but it also helps us connect with how he is doing emotionally. Kids don't usually walk up to you and say, "I'm sad today." Instead, they will lash out at a sibling with words or they will withdraw and be unusually quiet. Perception reads the cues a child is sending.

In her book *The Passionate Mom*, Susan Merrill says there are four ways to increase your perception: Think, Engage, Listen, and Wait.[6]

Think: Pay attention to what is going on around you. How often do we hear or see things we don't really think about? We can easily miss the tears running down a child's face as he runs in the door and up the stairs because we are so engrossed in our computer.

Engage: Ask questions. Engage in your child's life. Dig into your child's world so you really know what is going on in his heart and mind. If you have an infant or preschooler, resist the urge to check your smartphone when you're pushing the swing at the park. If you have older children, ask them questions about how they feel about things.

Listen: Listen to understand. Resist the urge to instruct or fix. Your goal is to be perceptive about what is going on in your child's world. If your children are small, listen to the difference in their cries. Pay attention to cues in their behavior that indicate that they're tired, hungry, or even bored! If they're older, listen not only to their words but also to their hearts. What's going on behind their words?

Wait: Wait until they are finished communicating before jumping in with your own thoughts. Too often we parents jump in with our own ideas and solutions, cutting off our kids' opportunity to come to their own conclusions. Resist the urge to think for your kids, wait patiently, and let them think for themselves. Doing so gives you great insight

....

into your kids' thought processes and increases your ability to perceive what's going on inside their heads.

When we apply the antidote of perception, we are harmonizing our hearts with our children's hearts by looking beneath the surface. In the same way we would tune into a radio station on our car stereo, perception allows us to tune into a child's heart and mind. This antidote takes us from surface "perfectionistic" parenting to deep intuitive parenting.

Acceptance

Every human being has a core need to belong. We want to know that people believe in us, approve of us, and accept us for who we are. We especially long for this from our parents. Every human being has a core need to belong.

In the midst of mistakes, poor choices, or—as we determined earlier—progress, we need to make sure our children know they are still loved and accepted. We want them to know they belong to us no matter what. Acceptance doesn't only need to happen when mistakes (also known as progress) are made, it also needs to happen when our kids are just plain old different from us.

In considering accepting her daughter's differences, one mom discovered this: "I have personally been struggling with how much importance I place on my personal appearance. Then I realized I was trying to control my daughter's appearance as if she were an extension of me. But she's not. She is her own person, and I need to treat her as such and let her express herself in appropriate ways." This very wise mom looked deep and saw the danger of the direction she was headed. She caught herself being unaccepting of her daughter because she felt her daughter represented her poorly in the way she was dressing.

....

So how do we get serious about the antidote of acceptance? Here are six ways to become more accepting of your child:

1. **Watch your thought life.** Too often we think things about other people, our spouse, and our children without even realizing it. When we pay attention to our thoughts, we can actually push them in a different direction. The Bible calls this "taking your thoughts captive" (2 Corinthians 10:5). Pay attention to what you're thinking. If you find your mindset judgmental, remind yourself that you are working on being more accepting. We can actually push our thoughts in a different direction.

2. **Be careful of black-and-white thinking.** It's so easy to think that your way is the right way—or the only way. Your child may come up with a different way to do something. Sure it might be less effective or not as time efficient, but that is okay too. Work to stop labeling your way of doing things as "right." My friend Rhonda says, "Remember 2+2 = 4, but so do 3+1 and 4+0. There are different ways to get to the same result."

3. **Look for the positive.** When we can't accept something or someone, it's usually because we are only looking at the negative. If we dig deeper, we can usually find some positives about a child or about the way a child does something.

4. **Stop judging yourself.** Our judgments of others are often a result of our personal criticisms. If we stop putting pressure on ourselves to do things the "right" way, we'll also stop putting pressure on our spouse and our kids as well. Not judging ourselves and others is a crucial step to acceptance.

....

5. **Focus on the now.** A lack of acceptance can generate from comparing things to the past. *This is how I did it with my older child*, or *This is how it needs to be done.* Instead of thinking about how something was done in the past, think about *now*. Comparisons to the past always hinder an acceptance of what is.

6. **Reverse the situation.** Ask yourself: What if I were on the receiving end of my attitude and words? How would I feel? When we step into someone else's shoes, it can help us increase our acceptance because we think about what it might feel like to be rejected and/or corrected all the time.[7]

Love

It's one of the most overused words in our vocabulary, and it has such a wide spectrum of meaning. "I love peanut butter," is a completely different use of the word from "I love you" spoken at a wedding while making a lifetime commitment or "I love my children" even when we don't like them very much.

Love is a blend of affection, devotion, and loyalty. It is part emotion and part commitment. Real love — unconditional love — is hope blended into the reality of life.

We learn about love from God, whose love is perfect, unconditional, and never-ending. The Bible gives us a picture of how love is lived out on a daily basis in the "Love Chapter," 1 Corinthians 13, which is often read at weddings.

Love is patient, love is kind. It does not envy, it does not boast, it is not proud. It does not dishonor others, it is not self-seeking, it

....

is not easily angered, it keeps no record of wrongs. Love does not delight in evil but rejoices with the truth. It always protects, always trusts, always hopes, always perseveres. 1 Corinthians 13:4–7

Our imperfect children need to know that our love is never at stake. It protects, trusts, hopes, and perseveres. Without even realizing it, however, we sometimes parent with this equation: Bad Behavior = Withdrawal of Affection. It's a natural human response to conflict and frustration, but it's not a healthy one at all.

When God is the leader of our life, He asks us to deny ourselves and follow Him. That means resisting the way we *want* to react and instead choosing to respond the way God wants us to respond. There's a battle that happens inside of us between doing things our way and doing things God's way. When we let God win that battle, we take another step of maturity in our faith. We also get to experience a sense of joy when we experience the victory of handling things God's way instead of our way.

Let's take a look at how 1 Corinthians 13:4–7 might, in a practical way, affect the way we love our children each and every day. You won't be able to do it perfectly because we are all a work in progress! However, you can allow these questions to sink deep in your heart and perform a parenting love audit.

Love is patient. Am I patient with my child who is so different from me?

Love is kind. Am I kind when it takes my child twice the amount of time to do something that I think it should?

Love does not envy. Do I wish my child were more like this mom's son or that mom's daughter?

Love does not boast. Am I quick to share what my child does well or to hide areas when the child doesn't seem to measure up?

Love is not proud. Am I hesitant to share how I'm *really* doing or how my child is *really* doing out of a fear of what people will think?

Love does not dishonor others. Do I ever dishonor my child, demanding that child be someone other than the unique person God has made him or her to be?

Love is not self-seeking. Am I ever selfish in my interactions with my child?

Love is not easily angered. How much energy do I waste being angry at my child?

Love keeps no record of wrongs. Do I have an ongoing list in my head about everything my child has done wrong?

Love does not delight in evil but rejoices in the truth. Do I keep my mind focused on God's truth about my child?

Love protects. Do I protect this unique human being God entrusted to me even when he challenges my authority?

Love trusts. Do I trust that God has a bigger picture in mind for this child's life? Do I believe God knows what his or her future holds and I don't?

Love hopes. Do I hope and believe the best for this child, or do I dread what tomorrow might bring?

Love perseveres. Do I keep my mind on the future possibilities rather than focusing on the difficulties and challenges I'm dealing with today?[8]

· · · · · · · ·

THE PERFECTION INFECTION ERADICATED

If you want to give your children the freedom to be who they really are, it starts with you. You have to understand the Perfection Infection exists. You have to be aware of the damage Perfection Infection parenting can cause. You have to know the difference between excellence and perfection. You have to know the antidotes and apply them to your life so you can give your children the gift of being fully who God created them to be.

You can do this! Now let's get inside the head of your child and apply what we've learned. Let's look at the core identity questions every child silently asks and how we, as parents, can answer those questions in a way that gives them freedom to fly!

Leah's Story

Once upon a time I was a young mom who knew it all. I was really good at this whole parenting and discipline thing, and my kids were very well behaved, at least in public.

One fine day I took my children to a festival downtown in our city. Kathryne, my oldest, was about five. Charles, all boy, was about three. And Ashlyne, my third, was a baby. This particular festival offered some children's carnival activities including a Bouncy House. Now, I have mixed feelings about Bouncy Houses. On the one hand, it is very nice for kids to jump and play without much danger of getting hurt, especially when there are not many kids inside. On the other hand, multiple kids means lots of germs and lots of chance of injury. Knowing this, I somewhat reluctantly let my older kids get inside the Bouncy House.

I stood outside with the baby and tried to watch the older kids through the netting of the House. After a few minutes another child came crawling through the opening announcing to her parent that she was getting out because "Some kid is in there spitting!" I was horrified. What nastiness! What an inconsiderate child! What poor parenting must be going on for a child to decide to spit in a Bouncy House full of other children? Full of righteous indignation I leaned down to the opening of the House planning to call my children out. Of course I planned on saying (rather loudly), "I am so sorry we have to leave but it appears that some nasty child is spitting

....

in the House." But before the words could leave my mouth, Kathryne poked her head out and said, "Hey, Mom. Charles is in here spitting!" All my indignation fled, leaving me deflated and embarrassed. My child?!!! Surely not. I was the poor parent? My child was the inconsiderate, nasty child? As I called my kids out and moved away from the Bouncy House, other parents glared at me.

I'm sure they were thinking the same things about me that I had been thinking about them only moments before. I faced my son and took a deep breath. Fortunately I didn't lose it and yell at him (even though I was definitely tempted!). Instead I asked (in a somewhat calm voice), "Charles, why would you spit in the Bouncy House?" He looked up at me, seeming confused by all the commotion, and answered, "I wanted to make a puddle I could jump in."

A puddle, to jump in. He wanted to make a puddle to jump in. He wasn't an evil, nasty child. I wasn't a poor, lazy parent. He was a kid—an ordinary, normal, curious kid who wanted to jump in a puddle. He wasn't perfect. I certainly wasn't perfect. He was just a normal, little kid.

I learned quite a bit on that day at the festival. I learned that there are no perfect kids. There are no perfect parents. And I learned that I need to give grace, even when I feel as if I want to judge another parent for her child's behavior. Sometimes she doesn't have a bad kid. Sometimes she just has a kid who wants to jump in puddles.[9]

· · · · · · · ·

CHAPTER 3

DO YOU *Like* ME?

*I*n today's culture of social media, contentment isn't easy, but comparison sure is. If adults struggle with comparing their insides to other people's outsides, you can be sure that our kids, who are trying to figure out how they fit into this world, are doing the same thing. This is why they ask core questions like, "Do you like me?"

Kids ask a lot of questions. Just spend time with a three-year-old and you'll be reminded of that. As they grow older, however, they don't ask quite as many verbal questions. Instead, they "ask" questions through their choices and behavior. They say what they say and do what they do partly to test your reactions. What you do and don't do answers their questions whether you intend for it to or not. That's why understanding the questions and formulating a plan to answer them with our

. . . .

responses is so important for us as parents. Being prepared for the questions is one step in helping our children see themselves in God's eyes. Kids ask a lot of questions — but not always with their words.

DO YOU REALLY LIKE ME?

Sit in for a minute on one of Kathy's sessions, and listen to the way this child expresses her longing for her parents' approval.

"Dr. Kathy, my parents don't love me like I wish they did."

"I'm sorry you feel that way. Can you tell me what you mean?"

"Well, they complain a lot. I disappoint them all the time. They hardly spend any time with me anymore. I'm sure it's my fault they can't love me, but I don't know what to do."

"Tell me more."

"They tell me they love me. Sometimes I think they mean it. I can see it in their faces. But sometimes it just feels like they had to say it. You know? They're my parents. They have to love me."

"What else?"

"I know! I know what I wish. Maybe they do love me. I wish they liked me. That's it. I don't think they like me. Can you teach me how I can make them like me? I think that would feel good."

"Let's start with a hug." The hug was accompanied by tears.

Parents have dreams for their children before they're born. Some women first dreamed of the children they would have when they were young girls playing with dolls. Then, twenty years go by, and that's a long time to be thinking about the child you want. Now, since so many parents know the gender of their baby prior to giving birth, they have

· · · · · · · ·

even longer to dream specific dreams. And plan. And speculate.

Are the dreams harmless? Well, it depends. If we're able to adjust our dreams to match the real children, the vision we had was harmless. However, unattainable expectations and deep frustration can result if we keep trying to turn a real child into the dream child we had envisioned and that image doesn't match who he is. We have to be able to humble ourselves, leave behind "what we dreamed," and embrace "what is" as we get to know our children for who they are created to be.

We have to nurture the children we were given and not the children we wish we had. If we try to raise what we want, without paying attention to who we have, it won't work. It won't feel like love. It won't be love. It won't feel like acceptance. It won't be acceptance. In fact, it will feel like rejection. We have to nurture the children we were given — not the children we wish we had.

Is it rejection? Even if you say it's not, the question is whether your children will say it is. What are they feeling and experiencing as they do and do not interact with you? Beliefs drive behaviors, so it's important to ask this tough question, "Am I wanting to reject any part of my child?" If your behaviors are suggesting to your children that you are rejecting something in them, then some of your beliefs most likely line up with that.

Find grace for yourself. Many parents have heard their child scream, "I hate you!" as they stomp off to their rooms. Most children have felt rejected. So have parents! When we correct our children, we have to let them know we're rejecting their negative behaviors, choices, attitudes, etc., and not them. We do that by saying something similar to "Bethany, I love you very much, but I do not love the choice you made

· · · · · · · ·

to be disrespectful. Your behavior was not okay, and you will lose the privilege of watching your favorite TV show tonight."

We're compelled to love our children. We don't always have to love what they do. Unconditional love is best. There's nothing they can do that would cause us to love them more, and there's nothing they can do that would cause us to love them less. Ideally, they love us in the same way, without conditions. We can't make them, but we can enjoy it when it happens.

This is why the young girl talking with Kathy realized her pain probably wasn't over love. "They're my parents. They have to love me." It was about whether she was liked. Something was going on with her. For whatever reason, she wasn't feeling appreciated or known. Maybe what she liked, her parents didn't, and vice versa. Maybe there had been a lot of complaining lately. Unlike love, which ideally is stable and always deep and wide, "like" changes, but it should always be present.

DESPERATE

Children are desperate to be known. That's why they do much of what they do. They're discovering themselves and wanting others to discover them, too. They want to be seen and heard and known. "Mommy, come see what I did!" is heard often from a young child. Even my sixteen-year-old man-boy will say to me, "Mom, come listen to this song I wrote," or "Come look at this cool website." It's tempting to gloss over those moments or give an automated response. I'm learning to give my son the gift of being fully present. This isn't just about a bit of attention; it's an invitation to know my son—really know him. Children want to be seen and heard and known.

. . . .

The basic "need to be known" can actually protect a child from his parents' desire that he be a certain way. I may wish my child had certain abilities and interests. There's nothing wrong with that. But if the wish becomes an assumption and the child isn't really known, damage can occur.

How do you feel when people make assumptions about you? When someone assumes you'd like to go to a friend's in-home, buy-this-bag-or-jewelry party? When someone assumes you're an early riser? When someone assumes you're artistically gifted because your house is beautiful? When someone assumes your whole family would enjoy camping with their family?

Perhaps you've felt disrespected. Invisible? Rejected?

How do you feel when your friends find out you don't want to go to the party, you're not an early riser so you won't meet them for breakfast, you're not the one who decorated your house, and camping is the furthest thing from your family's desires even though you have two sons? Do you feel unliked? Like you don't fit in? Dismissed? Unwanted?

Should we be surprised then if our children feel the same way when we make assumptions about them? When we're sure they'll like working in the yard because we do? When we're sure they'll want to learn to play the trumpet because we did? When we're sure reading will be their favorite pastime so we keep taking them to the library and bookstores?

Your children may not doubt your love. They know we parents are supposed to love our kids. We almost have to. But do they doubt your "like"?

Just to clarify: There are always times we may require our kids to do something they don't like. My kids have never "liked" working in the yard, but we live on two-and-a-half acres so, whether they like it or not,

....

they mow the lawn and help outside on a regular basis. Some of that is about learning responsibility and stewardship. It's about building character. However, when I go out to weed one of our flower gardens, I resist the urge to invite my son to join me. I enjoy the sense of accomplishment weeding gives me, but he does not. No amount of wishing he loved it will change that. I need to know that about him and respect that in him.

However, if I need my son to help me weed because we're getting ready to host a picnic, I will ask, "Austin, I need your help weeding this afternoon. I know it's one of your least favorite things to do, but I also know you enjoy having your friends over to hang out in the yard. We need to work together to get this done so we can all enjoy the yard we have." When we know and respect how our kids are wired, it affirms the freedom they have to be themselves.

DREAMS ROOTED IN REALITY

Regularly thinking and dreaming about your children's future is appropriate. As we've established, for some parents, this begins before they even conceive their first child. Dreaming and thinking is essential because hope is found there. Goals and practical steps are birthed there. However, as you get to know your child, your dreams must be rooted in reality. If they're not, one, two, or three things will happen.

First, the dreams won't be realized and you'll be disappointed. If you're not careful, this disappointment can escalate to frustration and anger. Too often, rather than being disappointed in yourself for choosing to believe in unrealistic dreams, your frustration will be directed at your innocent child. This feeds his doubts about whether you like

· · · · · · · ·

him. Even if this has already happened, new, realistic dreams can arise, based on your knowledge of your child. He'll choose to trust you again, and he'll grow as his Creator designed him.

A second outcome is possible when we consciously or subconsciously refuse to let our dreams die. We have to be right. We must have our perfect children as we've designed them to be in our minds. We have to create our children in our image rather than honoring how God chose for them to be. When we push our children into our mold, they can break. Their spirits can shatter, and their own dreams can die. Confidence may crumble as doubt grows. Questions form, and answers elude them. They become paralyzed by the disparity between who they are and the expectations placed upon them. Do my parents like me? Do they even know me? Can't they see I'm not happy? Doesn't it matter?

Children who break can be glued back together. Unconditional love, hope, apologizing, asking for forgiveness, and acceptance can work over time to demonstrate that our parental expectations have changed. Time spent with our children to genuinely get to know them may be the strongest glue. If you discover you've been imposing your dreams upon your children, be assured it's never too late to turn that around.

A third possibility exists. Some children can't risk losing their parents' attention so they force themselves to accomplish what they weren't designed to do in order to please their parents. They're desperate not to disappoint. Even though the attention they receive may be intense, full of pressure, and directed toward a minor slice of their lives, at least they're getting some attention.

. . . .

These children pay a price, and eventual burnout is common. Then, when they quit pursuing whatever dream of their parents they've been working toward, they can blame themselves rather than their parents: "I'm such a failure." "I'm a quitter." Although this is easier for them to admit, it's unhealthy. They're taking responsibility for something that really isn't their fault.

It's also possible that their true talents may never be discovered or developed. They're so busy forcing a false strength, they may never know who they were designed to be. These children aren't living with integrity—when what's inside matches what's outside. They may not be able to describe the confusion or the internal lack-of-fit, but they will feel it in some way.

Grieve the loss of dreams and goals. Grieve what isn't.

Even this third reality isn't impossible to turn around. Anytime parents realize that their expectations are not congruent with who their children really are—even if their children are adults—the strain can be released. If you are that child who is still not living up to your parents' perfectionism, it is possible to untangle yourself from those expectations. It might be as simple as choosing to forgive them, coming to know yourself, embracing who you are, and then moving forward in life. It might require the help of a good Christian counselor to work through the disappointments and hurt of the past. Regardless of what it takes, it's not impossible!

So what's the answer for a parent who has a child who is not like the "imagined child" in his head? There are two practical steps to take: Grieve and Know. Let's look at these two very important steps toward freedom.

. . . .

Grieve

First, we need to grieve. Grieve the loss of dreams and goals, whether long-held or short-term. Grieve what isn't. Grieve what you thought would be. Grieve what you imagined would happen but that never happened. Talk to God about it. Sort through it with a friend. Journal your thoughts. You may want or need to cry. It's okay. Let the tears fall. This is about letting go, which ultimately gives freedom to both you and your child.

I've had to do this in several ways over the years. On one end of the spectrum was coming to grips with the fact that not one of my five kids loved learning like I did. I loved school. I loved to learn. I loved to challenge myself educationally. I graduated third in my class, not because I was trying to be at the top of my class but because I absolutely loved to learn. Not one of my kids got my educational DNA. They ranged from doing well in school (but not loving it) to just tolerating school. At first, I expected each one to be just like me, which included loving to learn, being involved in student government, and filling their schedules with extracurricular activities. However, when the reality became evident, I had to put those hopes and dreams aside and grieve their absence. Initially, I encouraged each child in the direction I hoped he or she would go, but once it was obvious my hopes didn't fit them, I had to accept who they were and embrace their differing perspectives about learning and school. Once I took the "school and activities pressure" off each of my kids, there was no question whether mom "liked" them. My acceptance communicated "like."

On the other end of the spectrum, both my husband and I have most recently had to grieve our son's mental health issues. Our dreams for him did not include a diagnosis of PTSD (post-traumatic stress disorder), RAD (Reactive Attachment Disorder), personality disorder, and severe clinical depression. We certainly didn't envision our son cutting himself, attempting suicide, or spending months in the psych ward at the hospital. This is not what we dreamed for the little boy whose eight-year-old face won our hearts when his picture was placed in my hand eleven years ago. We've had to grieve the loss and rejection he experienced by being given away by his birth family and spending nine years in an orphanage. We've had to grieve the lack of emotional connection he didn't experience the first nine years of his life that causes him to recoil at a loving touch today. We've had to grieve what we thought his high school years would look like with him enjoying all that was available. We've sorted through it with close friends, talked through it with one another, and cried tears along the way. This is not what we imagined—but it is what it is. Grieving has been an important first step in untangling ourselves from our broken dreams.

Know

The second step is to know. Know your child. Now that you've let go of what you thought would be, become acquainted with what is. Study your child. Pay attention to how she's wired. Become familiar with his temperament. Come to know her pain, what frustrates him, or how her brain works similarly or different from yours. God prewired your infant. He scripted your toddler's strengths. He set your teen on a trajectory. God has given you an eighteen-year research project. Ask yourself, your spouse, and your friends: What sets this child apart? Childhood tendencies forecast adult abilities. Read them. Discern them. Affirm them.

········

When I did this with my non-school-loving kids, I discovered many things. My oldest daughter, Anne, is an introvert, which means she gets filled up by being alone. She didn't pack her schedule with extracurricular activities because she needed time to be curled up in her room reading a book. Solitary activities refueled her emotionally. Initially, she frustrated me, but then I discovered she was being true to herself. I needed to know and value that.

My son Evan had a great group of friends and enjoyed his social life outside of high school, but other than an *a cappella* choir group he belonged to, he was not involved in other extracurricular activities. He participated in the school musical once and hated it. (What? It was one of my favorite high school activities!) Yet he was a musician who also needed creative time. He and his friends would write and play music together. If he was involved in too much at school, he couldn't be creative. My pressuring him to get involved in school activities didn't take this into consideration, but as I grew to know my son, I better understood his needs and I learned to mesh my desires with his.

As my daughter Erica embarked upon her high school years, it became very evident she did not enjoy the confinement of school. She disliked the feel of "busywork" as teachers tried to keep a wide spectrum of learning styles tended to in the classroom. When she began drinking and hanging with the wrong crowd at school (remember how kids don't communicate with their words but rather with their actions?), we knew we needed to do something different. We withdrew her from school and let her finish her high school education as a homeschooler by signing her up for dual-credit courses at our local community college. She thrived in the college environment where you go to class two or three

. . . .

days a week and then you're responsible for the assignments and learning. No busywork! Once I let my dream (of her walking across the high school graduation stage to get her diploma) die, I was able to know my daughter better, see what she needed, and step into her world. Oh, and best of all? I started liking her again! I felt that, and she did too!

Shortly after we adopted Kolya, we went to the gym as a family. Nine-year-old Kolya didn't yet speak English, but his smile spoke a thousand words. As we entered the part of our local gym where there was an indoor track, Kolya began to run. And run. And run some more. The smile on his face communicated joy as he lapped us over and over again. In junior high, we encouraged Kolya to run cross-country. He routinely finished in the top two or three runners, often finishing several minutes before the next group of runners came in. In eighth grade, he ran on a cross-country relay team that won the state championship. This boy was destined for running greatness. I envisioned many wins in his future and the possibility of athletic scholarships being offered to him. There was one problem though: He loved to run, but he hated to compete. Even to this day he loves to run for the sake of running, not for the sake of winning anything at all. When he begged us to let him quit running competitively in high school, Mark and I eventually agreed. I had to grieve that Kolya didn't like the call of competition. He didn't value using his talent to accomplish something like an educational scholarship. He wasn't driven to compete, and I ultimately realized that if I moved from encouraging to forcing (which I'll admit I was tempted to do to "save him" from himself), it would have likely robbed him completely of his love of running.

Our youngest son, Austin, is similar to his oldest brother. Musical.

. . . .

Creative. He never liked the confinement of piano lessons but thrives on playing by ear. The piano teacher in me wanted him to have proper technique and the ability to play by sight, but I eventually had to let my dream of years of piano lessons go. Austin is truly an artist who isn't limited by what's on the musical score, and I've had to come to know him well enough to support that. Immerse yourself in learning and accepting who your child really is.

Grieve and know: Both of these steps take time. There are no shortcuts. You have to process the emotions to let go and then immerse yourself in learning and accepting who your child really is. Your child may not thank you now, or ever, with words. However, I know from personal experience that the joy of getting out of the way and watching him become who he was designed to be is a powerful expression of thanks in and of itself.

A GOOD AND RIGHT DESIRE

Children need parents to have ideas and goals for them. They need us to expose them to many ideas and activities and even dream about their involvement in camping, tennis, music, art, gardening, creative writing, cooking, woodworking, journaling, and more. If we don't, they probably won't discover their interests, strengths, likes, and dislikes. And we won't know how many different things about them we could like. But we must not dream for them without them. We can't leave them behind.

It's okay to let our kids try many activities throughout their childhood. This is an important part of exploring and finding out their talents, likes, and dislikes. In addition to sports and music, we chose

········

involvement in 4–H to allow our kids to try all kinds of different activities. Cooking, sewing, scrapbooking, woodworking, photography, art, and leadership were just a few of the many things they tried. Some activities our kids pursued for a year or two and then dropped. Others have turned into hobbies and activities they still enjoy today.

What about quitting? As a parent, it's always difficult to know when to require commitment and when to let them quit. I've learned this is an easier decision when I really know my child. Anne took piano lessons for several years, but it didn't come easy to her. In late grade school, when she asked to quit, we felt she had given it good effort but it was time to let it go. She eventually found her voice and moved on to enjoy music through singing. Evan, on the other hand, was an incredible pianist. He played well, and it came easy to him. When he asked to quit, we felt he had just hit a plateau and we needed to help him push through it. We let him take a break for the summer and changed up motivation strategies when he started back in the fall. That's all it took for him to push through!

Most of the time when our kids have wanted to quit something, we've required them to finish the season, whatever the season may be. However, we did break that rule one time. When Austin was in sixth grade, he really wanted to play football. He'd been wanting to play for years, but we just couldn't imagine that football was a good match for him (he wasn't even one to tackle his brother at home), so we kept putting it off, hoping his interest would wane. He was relentless though. Since there were no junior high school leagues, we eventually signed him up for the league in town. He was so excited to start.

He came home from the first practice in tears. He hated it. We

....

talked through all of the activities that would take place at practice like running, learning to tackle, calisthenics, and more. We sent him back to the second day of practice. There were more tears on the way home. He began to ask to quit. Not wanting to raise a quitter, we said no. The third and fourth days were a replay of days one and two. By the fifth day, we were beginning to see physical signs of stress. He was biting his nails, tearful throughout the day, and fearful of going to practice. Mark and I talked about it and decided that nothing was worth the emotional distress this was causing our son. We needed to put football behind us. He left on day five and never looked back. I worried we would regret that decision, but we never did.

Sometimes we have to dream for our kids and encourage them in a certain direction. We experienced that with our football-traumatized child several years later as he entered high school. This time it was about music.

Austin loves music. By the time he got to high school, he could play multiple instruments he had primarily taught himself. He was starting to write music and get involved with the worship team at church. At the end of his eighth-grade year, he had to register for his high school classes. We informed him we were requiring him to take one semester of choir. That wasn't okay with him. We explained that he seemed to have a possible music career ahead of him and he needed to be a well-rounded musician. One semester of choir wouldn't kill anybody, and it would be a good experience. We held our ground in spite of all his arguing.

He started his freshman year and complained every day that first week about choir. He hated it. It was stupid. He was angry he had

....

to waste his time on that dumb class. We told him he had to do one semester and quitting wasn't an option. (Honestly, he almost wore me down because I was getting tired of his arguing!) He continued to complain the second week of school but not quite as vehemently. By the third week, he mentioned something they were singing a couple of times. Week four, he talked about a new friend in choir. By the end of that semester, he had signed up for second semester. Four years later, I can report that choir has been central to his high school experience. He has been a part of an elite *a cappella* men's group, participated in Madrigals, starred in a supporting lead role in the musical his junior year, and began leading worship at church when he turned sixteen. If we hadn't dreamed for him, all of that might not have happened. We lent him our vision, and Austin took it from there.

We must guard against a good desire becoming a ruling desire when we're dreaming for our kids.

After the choir season was launched in Austin's world, Mark and I evaluated why he was so resistant. Tuning into this youngest child of ours and observing him closely helped us realize that he is a child of routine who doesn't like change. He also doesn't like to try new things in front of other people. He didn't mind trying new instruments behind closed doors. Once he successfully masters something, he then shares it. Choir required mastery in a public setting. Understanding this about Austin was key to allowing him to be himself, but also knowing when to "require" a harmless opportunity that could help open doors for him in the future.

How do we know when our dreams are good dreams for our children? Here are four questions to ask yourself:

. . . .

1. Is this about me living out my own dream through my children? (Did I always want this opportunity but wasn't offered it when I was a kid?)

2. Am I encouraging this direction because I see a talent they can't see? (Can I let them try something and be okay if they like it or don't like it?)

3. Do they have *all* that is needed to enjoy this activity? (Remember how Kolya loved running but didn't like to compete.)

4. Is there a hidden reason why they are resisting? (Remember Austin's resistance to try new things in public.)

Author and speaker Paul Tripp points out that we must guard against a *good desire* becoming a *ruling desire* when we're dreaming for our kids. Without realizing it, a good intention can become a rule especially when our own emotional stuff gets entangled in the dream. Our hope becomes a disappointment when our children don't do what we want. Unknowingly, these are the steps we take from a good desire to a ruling desire:[10]

A legitimate desire for your children: I want my child to _____

Becomes a demand: I need to have _____

Becomes a driving need: I will have _____

Becomes an expectation: You should _____

Becomes a disappointment: You didn't _____

Becomes a punishment: Therefore, I will _____

Here's a time I experienced this shifting of my legitimate desire into a ruling need: I **wanted** my daughter to reach out to a new girl attending the youth group. I believed my daughter was confident in herself, and I've always had a heart for kids who are new. So this is a sensible and legitimate desire for me to have.

She resisted and complained about just wanting to be with her friends. Rather than listening, respecting her perspective, or calmly talking with her more about why I thought she needed to do this, I became **demanding** in my tone. "**You need** to be her friend. You don't want her to be lonely, do you? You **should** reach out to anyone new!"

When my daughter dug in her heels even more and said that I didn't understand, my legitimate desire quickly became a **driving need**. "You don't have an option here. This is the right thing to do! The Savages reach out to others." The legitimate want that was a good thing for my daughter a few minutes ago had become something I needed her to do **for me**. Do you see the switch?

When my daughter didn't respond as I wanted, I began interacting as if this was now an **expectation**. It was no longer a want or even a need. It was something I was now anticipating.

As I waited for my daughter to agree I was right, negative emotions began to stir inside of me. **Disappointment** set in. I was disappointed in her but also in myself for not being able to get her to do what I knew was right. Adding this emotional pain didn't help me calmly converse with my daughter about the skill I wanted her to learn. So I **punished** her with my anger. Let's just say that this was not one of my better parenting moments.

As parents, you and I have every right to have expectations for our children about the skills we want them to learn and the things we want them to enjoy. We know them and, from experience, we know what has brought us joy. However, we have to listen to our children. We have to honor them by considering their legitimate wants and interests as well as their developmental ages and stages of life. This doesn't mean they always get their way. That's not healthy. Nor is it healthy for us to always get our way. When you and I believe our legitimate "want" is right, we need to talk about it with our children. We also need to model appropriate behavior while avoiding moving from a good desire to a ruling desire.

We are now almost ten years down the road from that "ruling desire" conversation I had with my daughter. I've grown up a bit since then, and she has too. In hindsight, I now realize I was expecting something of my daughter that was more mature than she was. It was completely fine for me to cast a vision for her to keep her eyes open for someone new in the group, but to expect her to behave in the way that I would at age thirty-nine was completely unrealistic. My daughter is now a mom herself, and she reaches out to new people when she sees them. At twenty-two she's mastered that skill. When she was twelve, I was just introducing the concept to her. Progress—that's what we're looking for, and I can truly say we've made progress in this case.

Masks

Fake is easy today. If we're not careful, we can parent with a photo-shopped mindset, thinking things can change with the push of a button. Believing there's greener grass somewhere for us to find so we don't need to pull our weeds is also naïve and dangerous. Parenting is hard work, and we need to realize we will make mistakes. I tell women that every one of us will give our kids some reason to sit across from Dr. Phil. When this happens it's important for us to take off our masks and allow ourselves to be known even by our children. "I'm sorry. Will you please forgive me?" can go a long way in the parent-child relationship.

Wearing masks prevents us from being known and from knowing others. Not being real isn't healthy for anybody, including yourself and your kids. Vulnerability is scary, but it is the backbone of strength in healthy relationships. When you know yourself and allow yourself to be known, it's easier to know your spouse and your children.

I speak from experience. In my early parenting years, I was not very in tune with myself emotionally. If I cried, I did so in private. If I was sad, I pushed the feeling away. I was afraid to be honest with my kids about my struggles because I didn't want them to be burdened with them. Of course, when they are younger, this is appropriate. However, as they grew older, I missed the opportunity to be known to myself, my husband, and my children.

It wasn't until my husband experienced a midlife crisis and left for three months that I allowed myself to be known. At the time, my children ranged from ages fifteen to twenty-seven, and I couldn't fix this hurt in their lives. I could only cry with them. In this dark season, I learned the value of vulnerability. Taking off my mask allowed myself to be known and therefore enabled me to actually know my children better as well. If your children are small, begin practicing "being known" in your marriage and friendships. As your children grow older, give your kids the gift of yourself—real, imperfect, and exactly what they need.

....

Who Am I?

Children need to know who they really are, and so do we. This includes strengths and weaknesses not blown out of proportion. Their true identity, chosen for them by God and awakened and developed by you, is what we need to know in order to figure out why we like them.

Identity is defined by the question, "Who am I?" It's important because identity controls behavior. Who children think they are is who they will be. When they know they're creative, they won't panic when an English teacher assigns a unique assignment. When they know they're self-smart, they won't worry about working on a project alone.

Where do children get answers to the "Who am I?" question? There are several places, including:

+ What we say and don't say about them to them.
+ What they overhear us say to others about them.
+ How we react to them.
+ Relatives, peers, and teachers (but parents will always have the most identity power).

Here's what this might look like in real life. If my son walks toward me carrying what I think is a lot and I say, "Be careful! I said, be careful! Watch what you're doing!" he may conclude I think he's careless and clumsy. Now because identity controls behavior, he's actually more likely to spill or drop something. Because we help give children their identity, we must watch what we say and what we don't say. Both change lives.

If after walking toward me, my son doesn't spill anything and places everything down carefully, I'll want to comment, "You were careful and alert. Thank you." These are life-giving words. Without them, he remains "not careful and clumsy." Now when someone says, "Tell me about yourself," he can answer, "I'm careful and can carry many things at once."

Want to strengthen identity in your family? Try this exercise: Have every family member write down fifteen to twenty statements that begin with "I am." Young children can dictate their statements to you. Most young children define themselves by what they like and don't like. You'll see statements such as, "I like spaghetti" and "I don't like Marissa" on their lists. This is why, when they like or don't like something, they can make a very big deal out of it.

Have your children do this without any explanation, which would bias them. Then see what they include and what they don't. This can help you put negatives in proper perspective and draw out their strengths. It can be very enlightening for you also to make a list for each child. If they're old enough, have them make a list about you. Comparing how we see ourselves to how others see us is very revealing. These can lead to honest conversations—there is power in the written word. Ask questions like these when looking at their lists and your own:

- Is each statement accurate?
- Is each statement currently true? (Or did they inadvertently answer the "Who was I?" and/or "Who do I want to be?" questions?)
- Is the expressed identity more positive or negative? (When Kathy has done this exercise with children and teens, she's had some with as many as sixteen negative statements out of twenty. Of course, not listing any negatives isn't realistic or healthy either.

....

In that case, we're possibly in denial, don't trust family members to know the real us, and/or we're fearful of being known. (Kathy jokes with her live audiences that anyone who has all positive comments should add "#21 I am proud" as their first negative.)

❧ Is there anything significant about the order of the statements? (For example, if you're raising your children to put their relationship with Christ first, you might look for this listed near the beginning. If it's not near the top of the list, then maybe your goal isn't as clear to your children as you think it is.) You will also want to notice if eight out of the first ten statements are negative. In this case, they're prioritizing what's wrong rather than what's right. This might indicate you talk with them more about the things that make you unhappy or concern you. This may be why they believe you expect something close to perfection.

❧ Is their identity complete or narrow? For example, are there statements about their intellectual, emotional, social, physical, and spiritual selves? Are there statements related to home, family, church, academics, athletics, and friends?

Doing this a couple of times a year can be a fun way of keeping up with everyone. Dr. Kathy knows of children who were able to safely bring up new interests with their parents by using these lists and the conversations around them.

APPLY THE ANTIDOTES

If our goal is to eradicate the Perfection Infection in our parenting, we have to know our kids and assure them that we like them. Applying the antidotes is one of the best places to start allowing our kids to really be themselves. Let's look at how to know and like our kids practically by using compassion, perception, acceptance, and love.

Give Compassion

1. Give compassion to yourself. You are learning as your child is learning. Sometimes it's two steps forward and one step back when we're paying attention to new strategies of affirming our kids and really getting to know them. Celebrate when you get it right, and give yourself grace and compassion when you don't.

2. Give compassion to your children. Make an effort to let them know they've been heard and that their perspective is valued. Put yourself in their shoes when they are down. Resist the urge to disagree with them when they tell you about themselves or share something with you.

Be Perceptive

1. Pay attention to subtle cues in your child's behavior. What is your son communicating to you with his behavior? What is your daughter saying with her actions?

2. Pay attention to the activities, challenges, and interests that cause your child's face to light up. Make a mental note to offer more activities your child seems to enjoy.

Accept What Is

1. Rather than disagreeing with your child's interests or even ignoring them if they aren't your interests, embrace what they love in the

....

moment. Remember: With kids, interests can change with the wind. Not everything they are interested in will be their interest next year. Your interest now reassures them you not only love them, but you like them too! Embrace what your kids love in this moment.

2. Accept things about your kids that you would like to change. One of my kids had a "blankie" she loved. When she was in grade school, I felt it was time for her to give up her blankie, but she would not have it. I finally accepted that this was important to her and I let it go. She's now twenty-two, married, and a mother herself—and she still has her blankie. No one was hurt by that! Accept things about your kids that you would like to change.

Love Unconditionally

1. The Bible tells us to "love without stopping" (1 Corinthians 16:14 THE MESSAGE). Ask God to help you keep your actions loving the next time you are frustrated or angry. You won't do it perfectly, but you will take a step to being more like Jesus! Love without stopping.

2. Choose one word in the 1 Corinthians 13 "Love Chapter" to focus on, such as patience, kindness, trust, hope, or perseverance. When it comes to your parenting, focus on expanding your consistent love in just one of these areas.

DO YOU LIKE ME?

Max Lucado says, "Study your kids while you can. The greatest gift you can give your children is not your riches, but revealing to them their own." I'd continue that thought by establishing that we must work to be able to celebrate their own riches. See what's good about them more

. . . .

than the places they need to grow. Grieve our dreams, and get to know our child's dreams. When we're able to do that, we can celebrate who they really are!

CHAPTER 4

AM I *Important* TO YOU?

"Mom, will you tuck me in?" Those words were once a part of my every-evening routine. Now I rarely hear them. My sixteen-year-old man-boy lets me occasionally sit on his bed and talk, but certainly not every night, and rarely does he ask the question with words.

I'll admit I used to find myself frustrated with those words because by the end of the day I was usually just done. Done parenting. Done doing things for others. Done being on duty. Done. Done. Done. Maybe you're in that season of life right now.

Yet, even when I found myself frustrated, I pushed through my tiredness and tucked in my children, embracing them in whatever way was appropriate for their age and stage of life. Why? Because I knew

. . . .

that deep in their souls they were asking a question that I wanted to answer with a resounding yes: "Mom, am I important to you?"

THE IMPORTANCE OF IMPORTANCE

How important children feel can determine everything else. Many positive and negative behaviors have their roots in whether our children feel important and valued. Of course this builds upon the first question we explored, "Do you like me?" because if we feel liked by someone, we feel important to that person.

Think about this truth from a personal perspective. When you don't feel important, are you confident or not? At peace or not? Comfortable? Outgoing? Kind? Involved? Do you see how your actions and behavior are influenced based on your feelings of importance?

Kids who don't feel important are at risk for many problems because excellence becomes irrelevant to them. When they perceive that no one believes in them, they believe in nothing. They're more likely to be targeted by bullies because they appear weak. They're less likely to get along well with others, and sibling rivalry is common.

Friends and family don't matter, so pleasing them holds no value. They're also less likely to apply themselves, so studying for school is irrelevant. If we want kids to be well and do well, we must help them not to question their value. Feeling important is the energy for excellence. It's also the protection from perfection because they'll have value in themselves separate from their performances. They won't need to be perfect to feel good about themselves.

Of course, there is another side to this value. What happens if you feel too important? This "positional pride" gets in the way too, doesn't it? Having to be number one all the time can get exhausting. It forces us to put others down and to dismiss their accomplishments. It can cause us to be unteachable and closed to the input of others. Needing to be "number one" increases stress, because we always have to feel more significant than others. We only want to spend time with people who we believe are less important than we are. We can become very judgmental and, eventually, very lonely.

So what we find is that Goldilocks and the Three Bears are relevant again: we want our children to have just the right amount of importance—not too little, not too much, but just right.

KIDS DO FEEL UNIMPORTANT

During many of Kathy's student programs, she teaches about identity. In the session, Kathy has children and teens repeat out loud, "I am important, significant, and valuable." She drives home the point this way with Christian groups: "You're not more important than anyone else. You're not less important. You're important, and so is everyone else. God didn't have to make you, but He wanted to and He did.[11] That gives you value. Not only that, but He made you exactly the way He wanted you to be.[12] That gives you value, too. And Jesus willingly took your sin upon Himself and died in your place so, through faith in Him, you could be rescued from a meaningless life and find joy and real purpose prior to living forever with Him.[13] Jesus' sacrifice gives you value! Smile, and say it again after me: I am important, significant, and valuable." Smile, and say it: I am important, significant, and valuable.

Sometimes after this experience, the children and teens clap. Some are desperate to know they matter. They need to know they're important. Unfortunately, too many don't.

Sometimes kids hesitantly approach Kathy after her program with this heart cry:

"Dr. Kathy, could I tell you something?"

"Absolutely."

"Umm . . . I know I'm important. I believe you and I like knowing it. But I don't *feel* important at home."

When these young people come up to speak with Kathy, pain is written all over their faces. Sometimes tears fall. Sometimes they quickly turn and walk away after at last sharing their painful secret with someone. Sometimes they receive Kathy's hug and continue to talk with her before she connects them with someone who can help them, if appropriate.

Most children who talk with Kathy say they don't feel important at home or in their families. Some have also talked with her about feeling unimportant at school and in church. What about your kids? Would they say they often, sometimes, or never feel unimportant in your family? If your kids are old enough and you're brave enough, go ahead and ask them! Their answers will be insightful!

Not knowing you're important has its own level of despair attached. Knowing you are important but not feeling you are important can be hard to process. One of the greatest dangers of children feeling unimportant is they don't feel necessary, wanted, or needed. Then life doesn't feel necessary either. We can, however, change how they feel, even if they've felt unimportant regularly. In fact, we must.

Because feelings drive behavior, start by courageously examining your feelings and actions toward yourself and your kids. How important you believe you are influences your behavior. How important you believe your children are drives your behavior toward them. It's different from love. It's about placing an appropriate value on them—not just because they are your children but because they are people worthy of your best. They've been entrusted to you. Place an appropriate value on your children because they are people worthy of your best.

Sometimes, the reason we're not successful when we try to change our behavior is because we didn't work to find underlying beliefs driving our own choices and interactions. To do this requires humility (I may need to make some changes), courage (I may not like what I find), confidence (I'm surrounded by good people who can help me understand what I need to), and grace (I'm not a horrible parent even though I'm not perfect). It always starts with us, doesn't it?

LOOK INSIDE

Children were not given to us to meet our needs. But in even the best of families, we may put them in the position where they have to try every so often. Still, if they seem to meet our needs for a while, eventually kids won't be able to do what they weren't designed to do. If that happens, we will feel our kids failed us. We may get angry and take it out on them. This is a damaging pattern, so hopefully we recognize it sooner and sooner each time it happens and make a change. Children were not given to us to meet our needs.

What are our core needs? There are five of them.[14]

> **We need security.** (Who can I trust?) We tend to think in the ideal: *My kids won't disappoint me. I can trust them to behave and make me look good.* But how do we handle the reality when

....

our kids make unhealthy choices, talk back to us, and we catch them lying? We can't depend on our children to provide the security we need.

We need identity. (Who am I?) We naturally feel, *I love being a mom or dad. It's the best thing I've ever done.* But when our children disappoint us, we may not be so eager to broadcast our identity as the parent of those kids. Plus, we shouldn't narrow our sense of identity to our role as parents; limited identity leads to limited belonging. We're also husbands, wives, daughters, sons, friends, colleagues, and members of church groups! So resist that urge to use pictures of your kids as your Facebook cover photo in place of your own picture. Your identity needs to be yours alone—separate from your children.

We need belonging. (Who wants me?) We want to believe, *My kids will always want me. They'll want me around. Everyone else pales in comparison.* But in reality, our children will separate from us—because they grow up and leave home or sometimes because their disappointing choices put distance between us. Though children may actually still love us, it can feel like "They don't want me." If a parent's sense of belonging is only tied to his or her children because the parent has diminished other roles (friend, church member, etc.), loneliness can result. The pressure children will experience can be enormous and paralyzing.

We need purpose. (Why am I alive?) It's easy, but dangerous, to find our whole purpose in parenting: *I'm alive to love my kids and to help them have a good life. No one else can do that like me.* Although parenting well is one of the most important things we'll ever do, when we can no longer rely on our kids for our security, identity, and belonging, we'll question whether we can fulfill our purpose: I'm sure not doing a good job of this. They lied. I didn't raise them to be that way. They're not as fun to hang out with as they used to be. Sometimes they act like they don't even know me. I don't know my purpose anymore.

We need competence. (What do I do well?) We all have a need to be competent at something. Again, relying on only our parenting and our kids isn't wise: *I'm a good mom. I know my kids and how to help them.* When our kids make mistakes and we question our abilities because they're not responding the way we thought they would, this need goes unmet. We'll feel we're not as good at parenting as we thought we were. We can be devastated.

As important as being a parent is, trying to meet our legitimate needs in our kids and only in our role as parents puts pressure on them and on us. If we want to belong, we bring along our cute daughter to draw people's attention. If we want to feel competent, we make sure our son has an important role on the winning soccer team. We can even meet our legitimate need for belonging through our kids who have many friends and belong to many school groups. We live vicariously through them. When we meet our needs through our children, we make ourselves more like a friend than a parent. This almost guarantees an eventual rift as the pressure builds for them to be perfect enough that you're not disappointed and to play a role they were not intended to play. Wise parents stay alert to the possibility of falling into the habit of expecting their kids to meet their needs.

This is also where our relationship with God becomes so important. Only God provides us with authentic security, identity, belonging,

········

purpose, and confident competence that last. Only He can meet our every need. Our kids need us to find our value and self-worth from our relationship with God. Only through our experience can we introduce our kids to the One who will meet all their needs as well. If a relationship with Jesus Christ hasn't been important to you up to this point in your life, consider the importance of it now as you are influencing the next generation. Give yourself and your kids the solid footing of a foundation of faith that will serve both you and them throughout life.

Only God can meet our every need.

Children can feel like projects their parents are trying to finish or problems they're trying to solve—instead of children in the process of becoming.

When our kids are freed from the expectation they'll meet our needs, they can be themselves. They can risk making mistakes and changing their minds as they work to discover who they are. They can feel important in this world simply because they were "knit together in their mother's womb" by the Creator of the universe who has incredible purpose for their lives (Psalm 139:13). That perspective alone helps children feel vitally important.

YOU CAN HELP YOUR KIDS FEEL APPROPRIATELY IMPORTANT

What causes children to feel unimportant in their own families, and what can we do about it? Thank goodness there are reasons to be understood and practical ways to address the issues. As you read through the following questions, decide which ones are relevant to you and your kids. If they're not relevant, let them go. If they are relevant, try some of the suggestions we list or some you come up with yourself, liberally

· · · · · · · ·

sprinkling in the antidotes of compassion, perception, acceptance, and love as you do so.

If you think a question may be relevant and your children are old enough, you can talk with them about it. If they agree, ask them to help you improve. If they do so respectfully, they can help you change your habits. They may discover they need to make some changes, too.

Don't be overwhelmed as you consider these questions. Select the ones that apply to you and pass over the ones that don't. We are learning together to honor our children by wanting what's best for them and modifying the way we are interacting with them in order to keep the Perfection Infection at bay in our parenting.

Is my child a project to be finished?

When kids are regularly told to change, they can conclude they're damaged and unacceptable as they are. Sometimes children tell Kathy they feel like projects their parents are trying to finish or problems they're trying to solve when they should simply feel like children who are in the process of becoming. If you feel this applies to your kids, you can turn this around by:

❧ *Teaching them to change, rather than telling them to change.* Remember: With kids much is caught, so modeling the change you'd like for them to make is far more effective than just telling them the change you'd like them to make. Don't overlook the possibility of formally giving them a "lesson," or providing them an example of how to change. For instance, if your son answers his sister with a hateful tone, don't just say, "Don't talk to your

....

sister that way." Instead show him how you want him to respond
with the appropriate words you'd like him to say and the tone
you'd like him to say it in. Then follow it with, "I'd like you to try
that again."

❧ *Making sure you're not asking them to change something that can't
be changed.* This especially feels like rejection. At times, we don't
think carefully enough about our words, and we might imply or
state directly they should improve or change something when all
the evidence in the world suggests they can't. Once, after Kathy
told a group of teens how she eventually became comfortable
with her height, she had a boy ask her if her parents ever asked
her to get shorter. Kathy wasn't sure she understood the question so she asked this boy to repeat himself. Kathy said, "No, that
wouldn't have been possible." He then mumbled, "Well, they
ask me to improve my grades, and I think I'm a permanent C like
you're permanently tall." She was stunned by his comparison and
instantly sad for how unaccepted he felt. Be careful not to ask
children to change something that can't be changed.

❧ *Affirming them for strengths with specific language so they believe
you.* Rather than telling them they're "good," tell them what is
good—their accuracy, focus, efficiency, kindness, or honesty.
Use the word "because" to provide proof. This makes it easier
for them to believe you, and it's more likely they'll repeat the
positive quality in the future. For example, "You're important to
us because you're ours. You're our only nine-year-old son, and
you made us a family." After checking your daughter's homework, you might comment, "You're a creative writer. I laughed

at the end of your story because it really surprised me." Do you see how powerful that affirmation is? You used a noun so now she knows, "I am a writer." You used a specific adjective. She's not just "good," she's "creative." And you provided the evidence she's creative by saying the ending surprised you. This makes it harder for her to doubt your praise. When you help kids identify strengths, they'll feel more important and connected to you.

Does my child get the most attention from me when he or she is in trouble?

Children feel unimportant when receiving little or no attention except when they're in trouble. If we notice all of the "bad" and none of the "good," they might conclude they're just an inconvenience. When we only talk with them when they're in trouble, they view us as judges who don't care. This causes them to feel like they're not a meaningful part of our family, which diminishes our ability to be a positive influence on them.

If you feel this might describe your parenting pattern, you can:

+ *Spend time with each child for no specific reason.* This communicates that he matters. Being in the same room together, even if you're not doing something directly with him, also encourages him. He may not ask to spend time with you and he may not ask to talk, but he wants to do both. He may never say "thank you," but it's not about you being thanked. It's about him being known, noticed, and welcomed.

+ *Play together.* Playing together offsets the days when children do

. . . .

misbehave and we have to talk with them about their choices. Make time (you won't find it) to play outside, at the park, and with each other at home. Build a fort with them rather than just knowing they're doing it in the next room. Be the honored guest at their tea party. Ask your teen son to show you why he likes a favorite computer game. Shoot hoops in the driveway. Always give the family a new board game for Christmas and play it often. Remember that play is also beneficial for learning problem-solving skills, creativity, innovation, empathy, and developing strong character qualities!

Does my child feel I only care about the things he or she does and not how he or she thinks or feels?

If we only ask our kids about what they do and how they did, they get the impression that performance is all we care about and all we like about them. Without realizing we're doing it, we may put additional pressure on them and can make some children feel like their job is to perform and keep us happy and proud of them. They can then infer that's the only way they are important.

Asking about this limited slice of their lives definitely limits our knowledge and our right to speak into the rest of their lives. Are we really satisfied with that? Honestly, we shouldn't be.

If you see this habit in your parenting, try one or more of these strategies to expand your questions:

❧ *Listen with full attention, without the distraction of your phone in your hands.* Many kids like talking in the car because you're

. . . .

captured. You can't just walk away if they share something challenging. Kids also like sharing their thoughts and feelings in the car because you can't make eye contact with them. This way, they can't see and then remember the look of disappointment you might give them. Although you may value alone time and you're more efficient running errands without them, sometimes take them with you to capitalize on full-attention conversation. Anytime you are in the car, resist the urge to make and take phone calls. Inadvertently, this tells your kids the person calling is more important than they are and that's a message you don't want your kids to get. Talking in the dark can be effective, too. You can't see each other's eyes, and the dark has a calming effect. Tuck them in or stop by at bedtime for your older kids. You may not want to talk at this time of the day, but the truth is that kids are more likely to talk at night. Take advantage of the opportunity!

❧ *Ask kids what they think about things.* It communicates you care about their brain and their perspective. One child told Dr. Kathy, "When my mom asks for my opinion about a song on the radio or one used during church and she doesn't quickly disagree and try to make me change my mind, I feel more important. This encourages me to keep thinking and valuing my thoughts. It doesn't mean I'm not willing to hear what my parents think about things. Actually, it's easier for me to listen to their opinions when they listen to mine." Ask for your child's perspective and opinions.

❧ *Ask kids how they're feeling about things.* This communicates you care about their heart. Because feelings drive behaviors, we need to know about the feelings. For instance, you can ask, "What's one

. . . .

feeling you had during school today?" This can be a challenging question at first. You can use a list of feeling words for them to choose from. You'll find a list of words in appendix A if you need a place to start. (I make copies of this list to actually pull out and put in front of my son when I'm trying to help him tap into his feelings. I hand him the pen and the list and say, "Circle what you're feeling." I give him a few minutes to do that and then come back to process his feelings with him.) This can especially help boys, who have as many emotional responses to life as girls do but without the strong emotional vocabulary. After they identify their feeling, it's excellent to follow up with questions such as, "What caused that feeling?" and "How did you respond when you felt it?" After you've asked questions like these often enough, your sons and daughters may freely share their feelings with you. This is a way you'll know they trust you. Because feelings drive behaviors, we need to know about our children's feelings.

Does my child feel I take his or her questions seriously?

Kids can feel insignificant when we don't take their questions seriously. Many have told Kathy one of the most hurtful things we say is related to this issue. After they ask a question, we sometimes respond with, "That's not important." Kids tell Kathy, "The question was important to me or I wouldn't have asked. Shouldn't that make it important?"

It's easy to brush off what we feel are silly questions in the midst of everyday chaos, but it's important we resist the urge. If you can see yourself in this situation, try one or more of these strategies:

❧ *Answer positively and honestly.* When we respond with, "That's not important," it might be we're actually too busy to talk at the moment. Or maybe we don't know the answer, but we don't want our kids to know that. Or maybe it wasn't appropriate to answer with other people around. Maybe the child was too young to handle how you would normally answer the question. All of these are legitimate reasons, so why do we say, "That's not important"? It's quick, and, let's be honest, sometimes we're overwhelmed or just plain lazy. (Admit it, give yourself grace, and move on!) Instead of discounting your children's questions, tell them the truth: "Great question. I'll answer it later when your sister is in bed." "You're curious. Great! I'm not sure either. Let's research the answer after I make this phone call." These are both good ways to answer positively and honestly. Answer kids' questions as honestly as you can, even if you have to admit you don't know or have to put off providing a good answer.

❧ *Encourage your kids to ask you questions about your day and your activities when you ask about theirs.* Don't be offended if they don't have questions, but choose to be available to them when they do. (Availability is a choice. There's always something else we could do or others we could pay attention to.) When they do ask, answer with age-appropriate details. Look for opportunities to use these conversations to talk about how you deal with frustrations, things outside your control, difficult people, and your mistakes. When they hear you talk about your imperfections and struggles, they are more likely to talk with you about theirs.

·········

Does my child feel there are double standards in our family?

Children feel like second-class citizens in families when we do to them what we don't want them to do to us. A double standard won't endear our kids to us. For example, one of the behaviors Kathy hears about the most is interruptions. Kids resent it when we interrupt them when they know they're not supposed to interrupt us. If they interrupt us, we indicate how displeased we are. However, if they complain about us interrupting them, we far too often treat their complaint nonchalantly. It makes their conversations seem less important and it makes them seem less important.

If you find this dynamic in your parent/child relationship, you can:

* *Teach everyone in your family how to interrupt respectfully.* Simply touch the person's arm or shoulder and wait. When the person you touch makes eye contact with you, you'll know he or she is ready to listen. This is hard at first, but in time everyone will find it an effective way to get someone's attention when they are doing something else. Role-play this new communication tool so everyone has a chance to try it and see it actually work. Together, practice how to interrupt respectfully.

* *Apologize when you are wrong.* If you're not in the habit of respecting your kids, apologize when you expect something from them they can't expect similarly from you. If there are legitimate reasons for having different standards for your kids, explain the reasons. If there aren't, then work to be consistent.

* *Stop yourself before you accidentally disrespect.* One place I had to stop myself is in expecting my kids to do something right away.

I don't like to be stopped and told to do something else without some sort of a warning. I learned a five-minute warning was helpful and respectful to my kids. "Five minutes 'til dinner! Please be ready to stop and eat in five minutes." Or "It will be bedtime in ten minutes. You'll need to stop playing and help pick up toys in just a few minutes."

Do I allow my child to offer his or her opinions or thoughts on family activities?

Children tell Dr. Kathy they feel unimportant and unnecessary when we never ask for their opinion regarding what the family does and when we never let them do activities they choose. Strong-willed children especially benefit when we involve them and when we agree with their ideas, as appropriate. Constantly ordering children to go here and there and do this and that can cause them to argue and feel especially invisible.

Find opportunities to involve your children in some family decisions.

If this happens in your family, here are some ways to tweak your interaction with your kids:

> ❧ *Find appropriate opportunities to involve your children in decisions.* If you want to go out for Italian, you could ask if they have a preference between three restaurants. When wanting to have a fun family night, ask if they'd rather bowl, go miniature golfing, or stay in and play board games. As with anything else, being offered a choice is a privilege. If they argue, complain about the options, and/or take too long to decide, they lose the privilege and you decide. In the Savage

family, Sunday night is family night. We take turns deciding what to do. The agreement is that we respect the deciding member's choice and we embrace the time together. This gives everyone an opportunity to weigh in on favorite things to do. Find opportunities to involve your children in some family decisions.

❖ *Monthly, on the date of a child's birth, let him or her set the dinner menu.* If your oldest was born on the eleventh, he could make a request for the eleventh of each month. Your youngest gets the seventeenth if she was born on the seventeenth of the month. As they get older they might not only pick the dinner menu, but they might also make it themselves, if you'd like to give them the opportunity to learn to cook as well.

❖ *Say yes when you can.* Being told no all the time can suggest to kids all their ideas are wrong and/or we're mean. Saying yes is not only honoring, but it makes it easier for kids to hear no when it's the answer you need to give. Several years ago, I issued a challenge to moms on my blog to "Be a Yes Mom!" When moms took the challenge, they discovered that many of their nos were because of selfishness. That's not fun to admit, but it helps put this strategy in perspective. When you say yes, and your kids see you going out of your way to help them do what they requested, they feel important. Say yes whenever you can.

Do I expect my child to do too much around the house in place of a meaningful relationship?

Don't assume having kids do chores helps them feel significant in positive ways. It's true involving them as meaningful parts of family life is better than not, but it must not be the only reason children feel seen or important. A very astute ninth-grade girl told Kathy once, "I feel like extra baggage. If the closet was big enough, they'd put me in the back with the suitcases they only get out when they need them. I'm a babysitter now because they had another kid. I don't even feel like their daughter anymore. I'm just their live-in help."

If you've inadvertently fallen into this trap, you can:

- ❧ *Ask kids to do age-appropriate tasks as early as possible.* This is a way to protect them from feeling used when they're older. If they help out from a young age on, they'll understand responsibilities grow as they do. It helps them see themselves as part of the family unit. Just make sure you know them for more than what they can do for you. Need help determining age-appropriate tasks? Check out appendix B.
- ❧ *Balance work and fun at home.* Yes, there's work to be done: laundry, dishes, cleaning, yard work, and more. However, there needs to be fun at home too: playing catch in the yard, board games, or a pickup game of basketball. Try to balance work and fun at home.

Does my adopted child or stepchild feel less important than my biological children?

The issue of stepchildren and adopted children can't be put in a box. In some families, adopted children and stepchildren feel very unimportant and in others very significant. It's all about prioritizing children equally while they're with us. As an adoptive mother, I know that sometimes our kids come with baggage that is difficult to unpack as it

....

pertains to these core questions. You can do all the right things and they can still come up with wrong answers in their minds. Don't use that as an excuse to stop trying, but do recognize that kids with baggage may need extra help to get to the place where they can see themselves in a healthy, positive way.

If you are an adoptive or blended family, you can:

❖ *Resist labels.* Kathy's niece Betsy is adopted. When she was young, her great-grandparents introduced her to their friends as "the adopted one" to contrast her to her brother and sister born to Kathy's brother and sister-in-law. Wisely, Betsy's parents asked them to stop. They didn't want Betsy signaled out in that way. (They did celebrate her "adopted day" with a cake and a discussion of special memories, but on most days the fact Betsy was adopted was irrelevant. And within the family, Betsy is referred to as "the gift" and Andy and Katie, her siblings, are "miracles.")

❖ *Be united as a couple while loving and disciplining all children unconditionally.* Work to treat all of your children the same when it comes to expectations and accountability.

❖ *Without showing disrespect for their biological parents, don't refer to yourself as a stepparent unless it's essential.* Avoid the word "stepchildren." Refer to them as "our children" and not "my children" or "his." Remember, there's power in the word *our.*

❖ *Spend one-on-one time with stepchildren to get to know them individually.* Be yourself. Don't try to impress them. Through words and actions let them know you love and enjoy them.

❧ *Include stepchildren in tasks and games that require the whole family to work together as a team.* This communicates, "You belong here" and "We need you."

❧ *Ask stepchildren what traditions are important and incorporate them, if possible.* This may require you to change routines or traditions to foster inclusiveness. When Kolya became a part of our family, some Russian foods became a part of our lives. One of his favorite foods is borscht, a soup made from beets. We not only learned to like borscht, but we also began to grow beets in our garden and learned how to make the soup ourselves.

❧ *Don't act as if life with a stepchild's "other family" doesn't exist.* Listen to stories about things they've done with them and ask questions. Don't be afraid of the other set of family members or the love stepchildren have for them. Kids sense fear and won't respond well to it.

Did you notice none of our suggestions for helping children know they're valued included becoming a "helicopter parent" who has to be involved in all aspects of their children's lives? We also don't recommend you become a "lawn mower parent" who mows down anyone in the way of your kids' success. These roles don't communicate, "You are important" to children although you might think they do. They might communicate, "I don't trust you," "I can't live without you," or "You can't protect yourself. You need your parents to get what you need in life." These unhealthy patterns can create doubt and immaturity in children—the very qualities we want to avoid. Avoid becoming a "helicopter parent" or "lawn mower parent."

....

APPLY THE ANTIDOTES

The way we interact with our kids strongly answers the "Am I important to you?" question in their hearts. Each antidote is a practical tool to communicating importance:

Compassion

When we are able to walk in our children's shoes, it causes them to feel important. When their feelings are affirmed and not discounted, it speaks value to them.

Perception

Watch for "wallflower" moments in your children's lives, moments when they seem to shrink into the background rather than taking their unique place in this world. Your perception of their feeling of "being invisible" can help them move from feeling unimportant to important. Even outgoing kids have their "wallflower" moments, and a perceptive parent can identify and address those moments when they occur.

Acceptance

Your acceptance of who your child really is will speak importance to him or her. Affirm his or her strengths more often than you address the places he or she needs to grow. When they feel like you're their best cheerleader, your children will feel important!

Love

When we feel unconditionally loved by someone, we naturally feel important to them. You can never express your love too much. Tell your children—a lot—that you love them no matter what.

AM I IMPORTANT TO YOU?

Kids long to know they are important just because they exist. They need to know they are important in this world and that they are important to us. The more you and I understand that and make decisions that answer their "Am I important to you?" question with a hearty "Yes," the more we'll help our perfectly imperfect kids find their way in this world.

Connie's Story

*A*fter coming through the gate for our local high school's football game on a clear and cool Friday evening, people from our small town began asking my husband and me if we had seen our daughter, Calan, yet. Being fifteen years old, Calan had asked to go to a friend's house after school. From there, she went straight to the game. Therefore, I had not seen her since that morning. So the repeated question made me wonder what she had done.

As we made our way to our seats, many friends smiled and simply shook their heads. Whatever Calan had done was obviously entertaining. My interest and curiosity mounted. Suddenly our attention turned toward the field as our team scored a touchdown. The cheerleaders began to cheer loudly, and the band struck up a triumphant tune. Then I spotted her. Running down the sideline carrying a gigantic school flag was Calan. Her entire face was painted red and white, and she wore red pants with vertical black stripes. I couldn't believe my eyes.

My kid! MY kid?! A face-painting, wacky-dressing, superfan?! This was not what I expected. I wasn't sure how to feel. What would her peers think? What would my friends think? What would the teachers and administrators think? A friend sitting nearby read the emotions on my face and said, "She's a great girl who is very well liked. She hangs out with a great group of girls, and she is her own person unafraid of what others think. Other parents would love to be in your shoes."

Wisdom—just when I needed it most. I thought of my daily

prayers for her. Each day of her life I've asked God to give her confidence and boldness. I've prayed for her to be well liked and not to lose her self-assurance when someone dislikes her. However, my expectations in those prayers included her standing up for her convictions when challenged, wearing modest clothes rather than racy styles, liking what she sees in the mirror, and being thankful for the person God made her to be—not this display of superfan craziness in front of me.

As I sat there contemplating, I realized she *is* confident and not only stands up for her convictions but does it respectfully. Sweatpants and T-shirts are her preferable clothing rather than anything revealing. She doesn't feel the need to wear makeup to increase her likability, and she embraces the personality qualities God gave her.

My eyes wandered back to the girl running up and down the field looking like a lunatic. My heart swelled with the love I felt for her. I couldn't deny the fun Calan was having while being confident and bold. Cheerleaders and football players were giving her high fives as she ran past. Students were cheering her on as well as the parents. Teachers and parents alike were laughing and complimenting her courage. Everyone was having fun!

When my daughter does not live up to my expectations, I have to stop and reflect. Many times, I come to the realization that it isn't my daughter who needs to change, it's me. I need to change my own desires. When I truly consider the person God created, Calan far exceeds any of my own expectations.[15]

CHAPTER 5

IS IT *Okay* I'M UNIQUE?

*O*ne day at a restaurant, a friend of Kathy's observed a family with two kids—one of them obviously adopted (he was a different race). He asked his parents, "Why I not look like my sister . . . or you?"

After a pause between the parents and a long stare at each other, the father's response was awesome! "Well, because we thought it would be boring to be a family of people who all looked alike and acted alike . . . Plus, just like God loves and celebrates people who are different, we wanted to be able to love and celebrate differences every day with a special boy like you!" That little boy lit up with pride and, without skipping a beat, said in response while shaking his head in agreement, "I special! Jesus told me I special when I's a baby!" and went back to playing with his toy. The parents stared at each other, smiled, and kept on eating.

. . . .

What a beautiful display of celebrating uniqueness. We all want to understand that we are special. We're designed with purpose. We're unique, and that's better-than-okay! As adults we need to embrace our uniqueness and help our children do the same!

THE CREATOR'S DESIGN

When God created giraffes, He designed them to like the leaves of the acacia tree. This tree is filled with thorns, and God knew giraffes would use their tongues to essentially lick the leaves off the trees. Therefore, He made giraffe tongues long so that giraffes can avoid the thorns while maneuvering to reach the leaves. God created their saliva thick and sticky so it coats any thorns they may swallow. Their saliva also has antibacterial qualities, so giraffes don't get infected even though they're pricked often.

Camels were also created with great intentionality. They can chew thorny desert plants because their mouths have a thick, leathery lining. Sand doesn't bother them because they can close their nostrils, and God gave them long eyelashes and ear hairs to protect them. They can use their third, transparent eyelid to dislodge sand that may get in their eyes. Their unique gait and wide feet keep them from sinking into the sand. Camels' humps store eighty pounds or more of fat, which they can break down into water and energy when they can't find food.

God wasn't only careful and thoughtful when creating animals. Each of us—and each of our children—has been created by the same loving, intentional God. He knows why He created us and designs us with these purposes in mind.

KATHY'S STORY

When Kathy was about six years old, after a particularly stressful day at school, she climbed up onto her parents' big bed and told her mom she didn't want to be tall anymore. At six, she already felt too tall. She remembers standing out from her peers and not fitting comfortably in her school desk. Kathy was also clumsy because she grew fast. She talked with her mom about that, too. She didn't like being unique in these ways.

Kathy's mom talked with Kathy's dad that night, discussing how to resolve the issue. Clearly, Kathy's experience and intuition had told her she could trust her parents with her heart cry. And Kathy's mom didn't hear Kathy's comment as a complaint but as a concern. Her first thought was *"How can we improve her situation?"* That's the love in action that all children need when they become concerned about how they're unique.

Kathy was going to be tall. Her parents, both tall themselves, knew that. The only thing they could do was help her change her attitude about her height. But her clumsiness was something that *could* be changed. By the end of the week, they had enrolled Kathy in dance class. Tap, ballet, and acrobatics increased her coordination so she became less clumsy. Also, because only the tallest girl was allowed to be in the center of the back row of dancers, Kathy began to like her height.

All the way through ninth grade, Kathy was taller than any boy or girl in her class. She tried playing basketball, but she thought she was so tall she didn't need to jump so she wasn't a very good player. Dance continued to be something she enjoyed, and because her parents had found a solution, Kathy was no longer clumsy, and she was a successful member of drill teams and high school and college marching bands. Although her height wasn't her favorite quality, it no longer prevented her from relating well to her peers. Because her identity was secure, Kathy had strengths to rely on when forming friendships.

Kathy loves challenging kids to live long enough and be strong enough to find out why they are the way they are. That's what happened to her. It wasn't until she was older that she saw the way God created her uniquely as a very good thing. When Kathy taught second-graders, she was helpful among her colleagues partly because she could hang things from the ceiling without using a ladder. It was easier for them to ask her to help than it was for them to drag a ladder down the hall. The overhead bins in airplanes used for overseas trips aren't easy for a lot of people to reach, but Kathy has no trouble lifting her suitcase up into them. She frequently helps others. And when she teaches at conventions and in churches, people can see her no matter where they sit. Eventually Kathy had the confidence in God to believe there was a reason God made her the way He did.

Kathy's height is part of her uniqueness. She's taller than most women and many men. It's not a problem, though. Why? Because when she was six, she had a mom she could trust to hear and receive her heart cry. She had parents unified in their parenting. She had parents committed to love her the way she was, but not let her stay there if there was something positive they could do to improve her life. They brainstormed together for a solution to Kathy's problem. Kathy never felt rejected because her parents helped her change her attitude toward her height, which couldn't be changed and with her clumsiness, which they knew they could improve.

IS IT A COMPLAINT OR A CONCERN?

Kathy's parents did something important we can all learn from: They didn't hear Kathy's comment about her uniqueness as a complaint but rather as a concern. I'll admit I don't always discern the difference, but as a parent I need to learn to separate the two.

There isn't much difference between those words, but I think the word *concern* can be defined as "heart cry." Kathy used that phrase to describe her parents' response. They heard the cry of her heart. Discern the difference between a complaint and a concern.

How can we as parents better hear the cry of our children's hearts? There are three ways:

- ❧ *Watch your pace of life.* Busyness crowds out compassion. If you have too much on your plate, you can't slow down enough to really hear and tune in to one another.
- ❧ *Listen to the message behind the words.* Sometimes it's easy to get caught up in the actual words spoken instead of the message behind those words. One homeschooling mother shared that her son said one day, "I wish I had time with you, Mom." She quickly responded to his words, "We homeschool! You have all the time in the world with me." Then she caught herself and listened to his heart cry. "It sounds like you'd like some special time with just you and me. How about we plan some time this week?" His eager positive response told her she had addressed his concern.

. . . .

❖ *Tune in to the cry of your own heart.* It's easier to sense the cry of someone else's heart when you are able to identify the cry of your own heart. What makes you happy? Sad? What concerns do you have that you have kept tucked away inside? Identifying your own emotions will help you process the emotions of those you love.

HOW AM I SMART?

Among the many valuable things to understand about kids being unique is that they are smart in different ways. The way they process their world is a way they're uniquely distinguished from their friends, siblings, and us. We have in common that we're smart, but we're smart differently. Kids are smart in uniquely different ways.

Many kids will ask, "Mommy, am I smart?" This can be heartbreaking because it may mean they've been teased, got answers wrong publicly, or that an assignment in school is especially challenging. Imagine being able to answer, "You're not only smart, you're smart in eight ways."

Our kids are smart in eight different ways. Depending on their ages, several strengths may already be obvious. Each intelligence can be awakened and strengthened. Each can be used to enhance learning. Misbehavior can also be birthed in each kind of smart (e.g., logic-smart kids can create problems, music-smart kids like to make noise, people-smart kids will always want to find someone to talk with). Older kids can identify career possibilities according to how they are smart. All kids can determine how they might like volunteering based on their smart strengths.

Mark and I took our three youngest kids through the eight kinds of intelligences one Sunday night. We looked at all of the intelligences and talked about the ones we were most drawn to. We also encouraged one another in what "smarts" we saw in each other. It was a great family discussion that affirmed how we are all unique, but also helped us understand one another better.

Here's how it might play out in real life: If you and your daughter are both word-smart, you'll go to the library or bookstore together. You'll enjoy the art museum and craft store with your picture-smart son. Your husband will coach your body-smart baseball player and you'll go to the arboretum with your nature-smart grade-schooler.

On the following page are the different smarts along with an explanation of how each one thinks, what they do, and where they excel in academics with each intelligence.

To learn more, check out Kathy's book *How Am I Smart? A Parent's Guide to Multiple Intelligences.*[16] I've found it to be a wonderful resource. You can also purchase a survey checklist to help you determine which of the eight intelligences are each family member's strengths at www.celebratekids.com.

FAMILY MATTERS

A family is a wonderful thing. Every member has something in common. Every member is unique. We are the same, yet different. We exist together; we exist alone. We are beautiful.

Uniqueness is a good thing because if we're honest, we may actually struggle most with qualities our children share with us. These similarities often remind us of what we don't like about ourselves — our strong will, temper, impatience, self-centeredness. Oh my! Can you imagine if we were alike in every way?

....

Intelligence	What They Think With	What They Do When They're Excited	Academic Strength
Word-smart	Words	Talk	Reading, writing, speaking, listening
Logic-smart	Questions	Ask more questions	Science, math, problem-solving, asking great questions
Picture smart	Eyes/visuals	Add to their visuals	Fiction, history, art design, thinking while doodling
Music smart	Rhythms and melodies	Make music	Music, memorization (e.g., ABC song)
Body smart	Movement and touch	Move more	Athletics, drama, working with their hands, thinking while they're physically busy
Nature smart	Patterns	Go outside	Biology, earth science, history topics related to nature, categorizing
People smart	People	Talk to people	Group work, discussions, learning about people
Self smart	Reflection	Spend time alone	Deep understanding and clarity, opinion pieces

If we can value our differences, there's a special completion that occurs when we're with our family. It's like puzzle pieces fitting together, nesting dolls that fit, or books in a series. When we're with those who love us best, we should be able to risk revealing who we really are. To be unique and accepted is freeing. If you read *No More Perfect Moms*, you likely experienced a freedom after being encouraged to be yourself! What we're learning on these pages is giving our kids that same experience of freedom as they are celebrated for who they are and given the freedom to be themselves. As we value our differences in a family, a special completion occurs.

Making lists of how family members are the same and different can be revealing and helpful. We might also list observed strengths. Including extended family like grandparents, aunts, uncles, and cousins enriches the experience. Siblings may appreciate each other's uniqueness in ways that deeply encourage and surprise us. Conversations about each other's strengths and unique character traits may help us see strengths or influences in us and in others that we haven't noticed previously.

Has your child with Tourette's helped siblings and grandparents be more accepting of others? Has your child with ADHD helped you be less judgmental when you assume other children in restaurants are just misbehaving and their mom is lazy? Does your gifted and curious son, who asks more questions than you can answer, give you hope that his generation will solve many problems? Does your steady and quiet daughter's behavior remind you to have a quiet time every once in a while? Is your nonathletic son able to admit he enjoys cheering for his brother from the sidelines even though he wishes he could have made the team?

Does a sibling mention nine ways his adopted sister is similar to him? Does a cousin point out how much your daughter with Down syndrome has matured lately? Does an aunt provide specific encouragement about the artistic creativity of your nonverbal son with autism? Does it then dawn on all of you that he's more creative than any of you and you start thinking of him that way? Remind one another that each family member is "wonderfully made" by God.

Seeing one another through a different lens does wonders for increasing appreciation of our unique contributions to this world. Remind yourself and your children that each person is "wonderfully made" by a God who "knit us together" (Psalm 139:13–14) and has a plan for our lives (Jeremiah 29:11).

HANDS AND FEET

For uniqueness to be appreciated and celebrated, differences must be seen as normal and, well, *different*. Not right and wrong. Not better than or worse than. Instead, we're all part of God's perfect purpose. This is confirmed in 1 Corinthians 12:4–27:

> There are different kinds of gifts, but the same Spirit distributes them. There are different kinds of service, but the same Lord. There are different kinds of working, but in all of them and in everyone it is the same God at work. . . .
>
> Just as a body, though one, has many parts, but all its many parts form one body, so it is with Christ. . . . Now if the foot should say, "Because I am not a hand, I do not belong to the body," it would not for that reason stop being part of the body. And if the ear should say, "Because I am not an eye, I do not belong to the body," it would not for that reason stop being part of the body. If the whole body were an eye, where would the sense of hearing be? If the whole body were an ear, where would the sense of smell be? But in fact God has placed the parts in the body, every one of them, just as he wanted them to be. If they were all one part, where would the body be? As it is, there are many parts, but one body.
>
> The eye cannot say to the hand, "I don't need you!" And the head cannot say to the feet, "I don't need you!" On the contrary, those parts of the body that seem to be weaker are indispensable, and the parts that we think are less honorable we treat with special

....

honor. And the parts that are unpresentable are treated with special modesty, while our presentable parts need no special treatment. But God has put the body together, giving greater honor to the parts that lacked it, so that there should be no division in the body, but that its parts should have equal concern for each other. If one part suffers, every part suffers with it; if one part is honored, every part rejoices with it.

Now you are the body of Christ, and each one of you is a part of it.

We all have a part in God's perfect purpose.

When children believe they are an important, essential, and planned part of their family and their world, they don't need to hide how they're unique and they'll more confidently engage with others. They'll more likely believe the best for themselves and others—that they will be accepted. Because they'll learn judging others isn't appropriate, they'll also notice how they're similar to others and not just different.

Although children act as if their peers are the most important factor in helping them feel comfortable with themselves, we actually are. If we as parents don't accept them, they'll keep looking for someone who will. When we do accept our children, they aren't as desperate to fit in with their peers. If we don't accept them, our children may compromise themselves to fit in and they may try to hide from their own uniqueness. Parental acceptance is more essential than peer acceptance.

Parental acceptance is more essential than peer acceptance.

Our job is to help our kids discover their unique contribution to this world. We all have specific traits, talents, learning styles, and temperaments that God longs to use for His purposes. The more we can help our kids understand we're all unique because we all have a special role to play in God's family, the sooner they're able to embrace their unique traits and put them to good use. Even if, like Kathy, they're taller than every other kid in the class.

APPLY THE ANTIDOTES

Our kids are in the process of becoming. They are exploring, discovering, and even dealing with disappointments as they learn their strengths but also their weaknesses. In this process they will come face-to-face with their imperfections, and we need to be prepared to help them process that too. Keeping our four antidotes at the forefront of our minds helps our kids embrace who they are without getting entangled in the Perfection Infection.

Compassion

Have compassion as your kids "become" all that God has created them to be. They will have high points when they discover they're good at something. They will have low points when they discover they're not perfect and not so good at some things. Helping them embrace both ends of this spectrum requires compassion, empathy, and large doses of patience. Helping children embrace both strengths and weaknesses requires compassion, empathy, and patience.

Perception

Kids are not likely to explore different activities without the help of Mom and Dad. Pay attention to your children's "bent." Are they artistic?

....

Logical? Technical? Are they drawn to details or to the big picture? What kinds of things do they notice? Ask for? See in others? When you begin to perceive patterns in your child's personality and talents, offer different facets of experience for them to explore. For instance when we discovered our daughter was artistic, we encouraged her to try drawing, painting, photography, pottery, glassblowing, graphic design, and more! In that process she learned what she liked and did well and what she didn't like and wasn't quite so talented at doing.

Acceptance

When your children identify activities they like or don't like, accept their opinions and feedback. Resist the urge to push a square peg into a round hole. This may mean that you have to deal with disappointment on your part if their interests or talents are not in line with what you were thinking or hoping. Remember, you're not raising the "imagined child." You're raising a real child. The sooner you can accept a child's uniqueness, the sooner he can accept it himself.

Love

Love is patient and kind. Your children may be impatient as they try new things. They may not like the feeling of not being able to be proficient at something right away. It's possible they will lash out at you in frustration over how they are unique. Resist the urge to mirror their frustrated or disappointed emotions and choose instead to respond in a kind and loving manner.

WHAT ABOUT YOU?

What's your story? Have you shared it with your children? They'll benefit. Like Kathy struggled with her height, is there something you struggled with as a child that you now see as good? Did you reach out to someone who helped you, or were you able to independently grow in gratitude? What role did compassion, perception, acceptance, and love play in your growth? Share how your smarts contribute to your uniqueness. Did this uniqueness affect you when you were young? Sharing will help your children know you better and help them find a sense of connection with you as they explore their unique traits.

Laura's Story

She said she had brushed her hair and didn't want to do it again. Observation made the statement dubious. "Mooommm! It's only hair." She had been playing worm with her sister under piles of blankets. She was wearing green fleece pants with penguins on it, the ones she claims are *not* PJ pants. Her top was a green ruffle tee (a green that clashed with the pants), and her shoes were black, lace-up boots. Her appearance made me squirm when I thought of taking her to the store.

I am not a fashion gal. I could be a candidate for a fashion makeover show where they stop an exhausted mom on the street and help her dress better. Still, I found myself embarrassed and apologetic when I took my mismatched daughter places. Do moms of boys struggle with such things? "She dressed herself," I whispered to a mom friend I ran into at Target.

I was never going to be a mom who harped on her kids to dress a certain way. If the situation did not require a dress code then surely I could let my kids express themselves. There are battles worth fighting and most days, if the clothes fit the season and are not easily destroyed by play, I wanted to be a mom who let her girls dress themselves. Lessons on first impressions could come later. Life itself would teach her that people respond to the way one dresses. Secretly though, I envied my sister-in-law whose oldest, at age seven, was

· · · · · · · ·

still letting her mom pick out her clothes. I relinquished the right to pick out clothes in exchange for peace when my children were somewhere around two. Many days, I found amusement in their odd outfits, but if life was grating in other areas, I wanted the satisfaction of having my daughter look nice (ugly truth: When life gets tough, I try to control the little things).

On a day when I needed control, I was arguing with my girl about her clothes. I was begging her to wear a cute, co-ordinated outfit. When she asked why, "*Because the penguin pants embar—*"

I heard myself. I remembered the embarrassed apol-ogy at Target. Such words did not belong to the philosophy I preached. Somewhere I had bought into the idea that little girls were better when cute, that coordinated outfits and bows and socks were important. Maybe it's because no one compliments your girl when she wears fleece penguin pants, but a coordinated Gap outfit equals three compliments from strangers. When had I bought into this fashion-driven culture? Why was I working against my own desires to teach my girl that the world looks at outside appearances but God looks at the heart?

Hoping she hadn't caught my half-statement, I re-tracted, "*Actually, honey, if the penguin pants are clean, they are good fall pants. Go ahead and wear them.*" I've since learned that style is part of my girls' personalities. I now enjoy the unique sense of style each of them shows. My girls'

. . . .

clothing is not a reflection of my skill at mothering. I've also learned that style evolves with age. A tomboy doesn't stay a tomboy forever. Neither does a girly girl.

There are times I set dress codes, like weddings. And some days I ask, "Do you care if you match today?" If they answer yes, and sometimes they do, I tell them that generally two different prints don't go together and that a print and solid would look nicer. Sometimes they shrug; sometimes they change. Either way, I never apologize anymore.

I learned these lessons a few years ago. Since then, I've found other sneaky areas where my words don't match my philosophy. I've come to enjoy that my girls express their loves and attitude with fashion (or lack of). One of my girls is a year and a half from becoming a teenager. I know this might get harder. That's okay. I think I've learned my lesson.[17]

CHAPTER 6

WHO *Am* I?

*A*t the core of all human hearts is the desire to figure out our identity. This is a God-breathed desire designed to draw us closer to our Creator. Since God created us in His image and with purpose, the closer we are to Him, the more likely we are to understand who we are.

Kids' names are important because they're the first labels they're given. If your kids don't know why you chose the names you did for them, share your reasons, especially if you named them for a reason or because the name held significance. Kathy's friend Jay and his wife named their son *Jamison*. Jamison was present as Jay told Kathy about his name's origin and how much he had prayed for a son. Although it's pronounced with a short i sound, his name means "Jay my son."

....

Although Jamison already knew the story, you should have seen his face while his dad explained it to Kathy. The connection between the father and son was beautiful and obvious.

Apart from the names we're given at birth, this world is full of labels. These labels often confirm or confuse our understanding of identity. Positive labels keep the Perfection Infection at bay as we learn to see ourselves as contributors to this world. Negative labels can contribute to the Perfection Infection in our lives when an inadvertent label seems to indicate we "don't measure up." In this chapter, we'll explore how to we can help our children understand who they are by applying positive labels without getting tripped up by the negative labels of this world.

IDENTITY CONTROLS BEHAVIOR

Kathy has worked with a trainer at One on One Fitness since 2007. On one particular day, probably when Kathy was struggling to handle the weight assigned, her trainer encouraged her, "Come on, Power Woman. You can do it!"

It's become a fun label they use. When Kathy's tired and hesitant near the end of a rotation, Linda reminds her she is Power Woman. Sometimes, when Kathy doubts her trainer's decision to have her do something, she confidently proclaims, "I am Power Woman!" as she grabs the weights. Obviously, sometimes labels can help us.

Pastor and author Craig Groeschel tells the story of getting to know Amy, the college student he eventually married. He liked her quick wit and sharp mind and was surprised when she described herself as an average student. Amy explained she had always been told she was average. She earned mostly Bs and a few Cs. After Craig got to know

....

her better, he asked her to believe him when he said, "God did not make you average. You have greatness inside of you. It's time to act like it."[18] She began the next semester as Amy the Brilliant instead of Amy the Average and earned all As. She earned all As for the rest of her college studies. What changed? Someone believed in her and helped her claim a new, accurate identity. She'd received a new label that helped her, instead of hurting her.

Labels communicate our identity to ourselves and others. They can be true and helpful or false and limiting. Sometimes we choose labels for ourselves. They can also be assigned to us by supporters, by people we can trust who are just wrong, and by people we should never trust. The same is true for children. Teaching our kids the difference between these categories of people can help them discern truth.

Amy went into college believing a false identity label, and it held her back from confident learning. You can see that it's essential for our kids to have true, accurate, and current views of themselves. This can be one of the advantages of listing twenty "I am" statements, as recommended in chapter 3. This is a great exercise for uncovering the way your children see themselves. You can learn whether your kids are believing lies—perceptions of themselves that are inaccurate or outdated. If they are, you can ask them where they picked up those inaccurate ideas. You might discover your youngest has a negative teacher or your oldest is remembering something you said two years ago.

THE MIRACLE IDENTITY

As we shared in the last chapter, our uniqueness is a good thing. One label we wish every child (and adult!) believed is this: "I'm a unique,

. . . .

one-of-a-kind, unrepeatable miracle!" Even kids who have labels in common are still unique from each other. Kids who are the oldest in their families share that label, but not everything else. Kids who share "I have epilepsy" as a label are unique in other ways. The differences connect them to others but also give them freedom to discover their whole selves when they know they are one-of-a-kind miracles! "I'm a unique, one-of-a-kind, unrepeatable miracle!"

Kids who know they're miracles are empowered. They understand God wanted them to exist. They're not mistakes. Kathy has found teaching this identity to kids of all ages frees them to work through and past their concerns, anxieties, pressures, and even depression. It increases their hope for the future. She reminds them to remember they're miracles when they're questioning their value and wondering whether they are mistakes instead.

You may be surprised to learn that seeing themselves as miracles is also empowering for kids with permanent and temporary medical issues such as ADHD, ODD, Autism Spectrum Disorder, a cancer diagnosis, depression, and anxiety disorders. We need to remember our kids are more than any label that describes them. They can know it, too, when we talk with them about the rest of who they are. We don't introduce them to everyone as "this is the one who has [whatever diagnosed issue]." Our children need to know we know them more than we know their illness. We see them before we see the illness. That disease or disorder is a part of their miracle identity. It's not a mistake.

In the Savage family all kinds of labels have been thrown around over the years: Oldest, youngest, and middle child. Adopted. ADHD. Anxious. Prodigal. Smart. Thinker. Feeler. Introvert. Extrovert. Talker.

....

Quiet. Internal Processor. External Processor. Verbal. Funny. Entertaining. Difficult. Easy. Rebel. Strong-willed. These labels are intended to describe both the strengths as well as the struggles the various members of our family have. Admittedly, however, we've probably not been as good about protecting our family from easy-to-assign labels that too often can hurt rather than help. It's just been in recent years that I've really been convicted of measuring my words more carefully. Maybe you feel similarly convicted. It's never too late, though. You can start using positive labels today, no matter how old your kids are!

When Kathy and members of her staff run into teens they taught years ago, the young people will often spontaneously smile and recite, "I'm a unique, one-of-a-kind, unrepeatable miracle!" Then they testify that they've abstained from drugs and alcohol because their brain cells are theirs and no one else's and they don't want them ruined. Their future is theirs and no one else's. Their dreams, goals, ambitions, and hopes are theirs and no one else's. They're alive, they didn't have to be created, and they don't want to waste God's decision. Obviously, the label of "unique miracle" can even be lifesaving.

"DOING" LABELS

Many labels are earned because of what kids do. That's understandable and can be positive. These include statements such as "I am an athlete." Often kids will include a descriptive adjective — "a good athlete." In most cases, we give them those adjectives either in conversation as we introduce them to others or in the way we react to them. However, it's important that we realize both ends of the spectrum when it comes to "doing labels"—that is, labels that are closely associated with what our kids do. One end of the spectrum motivates; the other end of the spectrum can end up in pride.

For instance, "I'm a star athlete" can be positive, as it motivates kids to practice and listen carefully to their coaches so they maintain their excellence. But it can make teamwork challenging if the "star athlete" becomes prideful and sets himself up as better than his peers.

"I'm a terrible singer" is obviously a negative way for your daughter to declare she's not singing well. You might help her realign her thinking by a comment such as, "You may not be singing well at the moment, but that doesn't make you a terrible singer. We all have bad days, and we can use those to motivate us to keep practicing or work at a particular skill." Her frustration can be positive if it's short-lived and it motivates her to practice and work at a particular skill she's lacking. But the "I'm a terrible singer" statement can be negative if it causes her to give up. It's also negative if she draws this conclusion just by comparing herself to the best singers in her choir.

It's best when "doing" identities are specific descriptions of behavior rather than general statements. For instance, it would be better for your daughter to know, "I've got to figure out how to make my breaths last longer. And I know my director is right. I need to practice singing the scales." She's identifying specific skills to work on so she won't feel "terrible" anymore. Your son who thinks of himself as a "bad writer" would be better off describing his specific goals: "I need to remember to proofread to add more adjectives to my essays to make my writing richer." In this way his label becomes "I'm choosing to improve my writing."

Not all good athletes are the same. When your kids know what makes them uniquely good, they'll know how they can specifically help a team or help a less-skilled player. They'll also know what they weren't able to list as part of their skills that they could work on more. For instance, your son might be able to identify his talent in this way: "I'm better at football this year because I worked on speed and agility over the summer." Your soccer-playing daughter might state, "I'm playing well this year because I'm looking ahead better to predict where the defensive players are going." Identity controls behavior.

Because identity controls behavior, you'll want your kids to have "doing identities" for the activities they value and for activities you want them to value. For example, if they have the athlete identity but not an "I'm a learner" identity, this will explain why they don't prioritize studying.

Consider how our words matter. "I'm a learner" identity is healthier than "I'm a student." Students study. Learners learn. Learning should take place all the time and includes life and topics not covered in school. Thinking of oneself as a student can be a bit limiting, but a "learner" label can be beneficial throughout our entire lives. My friend Pam and her husband, Bill, did something every August before school started in order to call out the learner and leader in their kids. They called it their "Learner/Leader" conversation. Our words matter.

Positive labels help our kids know and verbalize their strengths.

To this day, I identify myself as a learner. One of my favorite conferences to attend, besides the Hearts at Home conferences we do for moms, is the Willow Creek Leadership Summit. I furiously take notes at every session, and I always walk away equipped and encouraged as a leader. When I attend sessions at the Hearts at Home conferences (yes, I lead sessions, but I also attend them!), I walk away feeling like I understand marriage, parenting, homemaking, or whatever the topic better than I did before I attended the session.

What "doing" labels are important to you that you'd love your kids to embrace? What are you doing so it happens?

"I am a reader."

"I like exploring and figuring things out."

"I'm an artist."

"I play the piano."

"I like exercise."

"I take good care of my pets."

"I volunteer at my grandma's nursing home."

"I collect money and used toys for our local women's shelter."

Whatever positive "doing labels" we can help our kids say about themselves will help them know and verbalize their strengths. They will also offset the weaknesses, which we often seem to elevate in our minds. "Doing" labels identify interests, skills, and strengths that help us see how God is using us in this world.

"BEING" LABELS

Kids will naturally own "doing" labels, but their "being" labels are even more important. We're human *beings*, not human *doings*. Who we are causes us to do what we do.

Listen and look to see who your kids are being and specifically affirm what you notice. "You are being kind to your brother."

"You are patient while we're waiting. Thank you."

"You are compassionate. I'm glad you went to see if your friend is okay."

"You were obedient this morning."

"I love your joy!"

"You're a loyal friend. I like how you remembered to talk with your quiet classmate."

"You are comfortable being alone. I'm glad because it helps me spend quality time with your grandpa."

"You are clever. What a great solution!"

"You are fun to spend time with."

These "being" labels are character-building for your kids. They affirm who they are becoming on the inside. God's far more interested in who we are becoming than in what we are doing. When we understand that ourselves, we can better help our kids understand that too.

When you talk with your kids about school, in addition to asking, "What's one interesting thing you did or learned today?" ask "Who were you in school today?" The first time you ask this, your kids are bound to look at you funny, but you want them to start thinking in these terms. Were they the kind and compassionate children you're raising them to be or mean and self-centered? Sometimes it's the things not on the report card or the daily web-based reports from teachers that you most need to know. When we tweak the questions we ask, we help our children identify character strengths we want them to be aware of.

When you provide a three-prong affirmation, there's a greater chance these qualities you admire will become identities forming your kids' essence. Don't overuse this formula. Perhaps use it for the one to two "being" qualities you most want to instill in them now. Remember Goldilocks: not too much, not too little, but just right. Use, but don't overuse, the three-prong affirmation.

This is what a three-prong affirmation looks like:

1. "You are _____." (Verbalize a specific positive quality you've observed.)
2. "I know because _____." (Provide the evidence you've seen and/or heard the behavior. This makes it easier for them to believe you. "Because" is one of your power words. It forces you to find specifics to affirm, and it strengthens your influence.)
3. "I'm glad because _____." (The reason you're glad your kids have this quality can motivate them to keep being it. You're providing the purpose, one of the motivators that drives excellence.)

Here's an example: "You are generous. I know because when Aunt Gina told you she was collecting food for the food pantry, you used your money to buy some soup when we went to the store. I'm glad because God calls us to put others first."

And one more: "You have self-control. I know because you could have whined and complained and even teased your sister when we had to wait for Daddy to finish his meeting, but you didn't. You're growing up and maturing, and I'm so glad! Self-control is important in order to be obedient, and you know your dad and I want you to be obedient."

· · · · · · · ·

THE POWER OF A POSITIVE DAD

If you're a dad reading this book, we're hopeful you're enjoying the first-ever Hearts at Home parenting book written for both Mom and Dad. The next two sections are especially for you. If you're a mom reading this book, the next two sections could be especially helpful to share with your children's father because his influence is of great importance in your child's life.

When children complain about their parents expecting perfection, we hear a lot about dads. According to many children, dads are often the ones who look at schoolwork and their athletic and artistic performances and say, "You can do better." They ask questions to suggest they're not satisfied. This causes kids to conclude, "I can never please my dad." This is a damaging identity for our kids that we need to avoid if at all possible. Dads and moms need to choose to be positive when talking with their kids.

It is a choice. There's always something kids can do better, faster, neater, or quieter. As parents, we need to think about whether the "problem" needs to be pointed out. We need to let some things go. Not every hill is a hill worth dying on. Remember the goal is progress, not perfection. We root out Perfection Infection parenting when we learn to address the things that really matter in this life.

When issues come up with my children and emotions get high, sometimes I stop and ask myself, "Will this matter in ten years?" I've come to understand if the answer is yes, then I need to fight for it, but if the answer is no, then I let it go. Sometimes moms and dads can make mountains out of molehills. We cause conflict that just doesn't need to happen.

········

Timing is also important in communication. In the years when I was a stay-at-home mom, there were many times I was in tune with the emotions and struggles our kids had dealt with throughout the day or even in the hours after school. Mark would get home from work and sometimes make a comment without taking into consideration the context of the situation. Too often this caused marital conflict that could have been avoided. Eventually we learned to talk when Mark was driving home from work. This allowed me to "brief" him on the atmosphere at home, the emotions of each child, which kid had already been in trouble several times over the past hour, and where he needed to be sensitive. This way when he came home from work and saw that the trash cans had not been moved up from the end of the driveway, he didn't walk in the door and correct a child who was already having a hard day. Sure, accountability was needed, but it needed to be done in the right timing, taking into account the context of what was already happening at home.

Dads, when it's appropriate to talk about the negatives, do so in an optimistic, positive way so kids know you believe in them and their ability to improve. This includes pointing out things that went well even when you're displeased about part of a performance. (We'll discuss this concept even more in the next two chapters when we look at failure and helping our kids change.) When you have to communicate about problems or weaknesses, communicate that you believe in your kids and their ability to improve.

YOU ARE BEAUTIFUL

Girls need their dads to affirm their beauty. If they don't, girls will look for a man who will someday. Often, they'll feel a need for more

....

than one to fill the void left by a lack of affirmation from Dad. Unhealthy relationships follow emotionally unhealthy girls. One of the most important labels for girls to identify with is, "My dad believes I'm beautiful." That's powerful. Girls can be cute or pretty when they're little, but they need to graduate to "beautiful." A dad's affirmation of a daughter's beauty is powerful.

Dads shouldn't overdo lavish praise about outward appearance. We know some men who walk into church with their beautiful little girls in a way that unfortunately uses them as trophies. A girl's label should not be, "My dad uses me to get attention for himself." Her beauty is hers. It's not for you.

Dads can specifically comment on their daughter's hair, skin, jewelry, clothes, and more. Specifically affirming decisions related to what they do with their wardrobe, hair, and makeup are most important because those good choices are repeatable. These specific affirmations become a good way for dads to communicate their values.

- ❖ "The length of your skirt is just right. I'm proud of your mature choice. It shows you care about yourself and being respectful of what your mom and I want for you and not what Hollywood says is right. That's great!"
- ❖ "I'm proud of you for not wearing too much makeup. You have nothing to cover up. You're beautiful just the way you are. I know you want to wear makeup, so I'm really glad you're just accenting your natural God-given beauty."
- ❖ "Sweetheart, I like those plaid shorts. You like plaid things, don't you? You're beautiful on the inside and the outside."

. . . .

It's really helpful when dads are aware of their daughter's worries and insecurities. When dads know what makes their daughters nervous, they can choose to speak into those situations. If a daughter thinks she's clumsy, Dad can proclaim, "The flow of your skirt adds to how graceful you look." If a daughter worries about her taste in clothes and is wearing something new, Dad can say something specific to encourage her like, "That shade of blue brings out the blue in your eyes. Wise choice." Or, "That's an unusual necklace. I really like it."

It takes effort to make affirming comments to our kids, but solidifying our children's identity is worth the effort.

Are these observations and comments natural for most dads to make? Probably not. This is where moms and dads can partner together because dads need to make such verbal affirmations whether they come easily or not. Many times over the years, I've whispered in my husband's ear things like, "Erica just got a new haircut—make sure you notice it." Or "Anne got her braces off today—she needs her daddy to comment on her pretty teeth." Of course, Dad's not the only one who sometimes needs these reminders. There were plenty of times when Mark would whisper something in my ear as well. "I just learned that Austin broke up with his girlfriend today. He's a bit moody. Give him some extra encouragement and grace." In all aspects of parenting, what we see is a choice. What we hear is a choice. What we say is a choice. What we do is a choice. It takes some extra effort to make observations and affirming comments to our kids, but solidifying our children's identity is definitely worth the effort.

If your daughter's dad isn't involved in her life, we encourage you to ask an important man to affirm her as we've described. These

....

comments can come from a grandfather, uncle, a family friend from church, or the dad of one of your daughter's best friends. Sometimes we have to advocate for our kids and help fill the gaps that exist in their lives.

Of course, dads must also tell their daughters they're more than beautiful on the outside. Physical beauty can't be the only label dads give their daughters. Following "You're beautiful" with other affirmations will assure their daughters have positive labels from each component of their identity.

- "I've noticed it's getting easier for you to remember your spelling words and math facts. I'm proud of you. Your memory is improving." (intellectual)
- "I appreciate how calm you stay even when people around you get tense. You stay cool and composed even when things get chaotic." (emotional)
- "Your great sense of humor adds to the quality of your friendships. I enjoy listening to you guys joke around in the den." (social)
- "I've noticed you concentrating and taking notes during the Sunday sermon. I'm encouraged by your interest in God and His truth." (spiritual)

Our words—both positive and negative—carry great power for our kids. It's important that we keep the negative to a minimum and get specific with the positive. Doing so will strengthen our children's unique identities and help them stand firm in who God has created them to be.

APPLY THE ANTIDOTES

As children figure out who they are and identify with both positive and negative labels, our interaction with them will help them resist the Perfection Infection. As you relate with your kids . . .

Be Compassionate

It's not easy to figure out who we are and who we're not. It's especially not easy to process the negative labels of this world. When your children express a concern about themselves, listen and respond with empathy before you try to help them see the positive side of things. The old adage "People don't care about how much you know until they know how much you care," applies to kids, as well.

Be Perceptive

When raising kids, sometimes the little things can really be the big things. If your children downplay something that most likely brought them confusion or pain, keep a close eye on their emotional temperature. Ask God to increase your ability to perceive beyond the surface of what is going on.

Be Accepting

Even though it's easy to teasingly slap a negative label on your children (especially those who fall on the far ends of the spectrum — very easy or very difficult), resist the temptation when you catch yourself. If a negative label slips out, counter it with several positive ones that let your children know you accept them and see them as more than any negative label. Accept their differences, their challenges, and even the

. . . .

struggles you have with them as a normal part of parenting.

Be Loving

You can never tell your kids too often that you love them. Be affection-ate and generous with the love you show them. In the younger years, you can never hug, snuggle with, kiss on the cheek, or hold their hand too much. As your kids get older, loving touch is no longer a part of ev-eryday life without intentionality. Be intentional with showing physical love by putting your hand on your son's shoulder or giving him a side squeeze. Be intentional about saying "I love you," whenever you can. You can never tell your kids too often that you love them.

WHO AM I?

Sometimes children feel insignificant and invisible because they don't know how they're unique and/or uniquely appreciated. Do you always introduce your children as a group, "These are my kids"? If so, you can begin to separate them by name and add adjectives or phrases when it's appropriate. It can be more than "my oldest son." It could be "This is Jack, my quick runner." Reflect on how they're unique in different categories we introduced earlier—their intellectual, emotional, social, physical, and spiritual selves. The more they hear you call out their unique, defining, positive traits, the more they will begin to define themselves positively too!

Christy's Story

My oldest son never did well in school. It wasn't that he wasn't smart; it was that school bored him, and the social aspect was too much for him to handle. He should have graduated this year, but he chose not to do his schoolwork for many years. So the wonderful, sweet, intelligent boy was not a senior, but started this school year as a sophomore and ended as a junior. Not wanting to further humiliate himself, he decided he wouldn't return to school and instead would get his GED.

During graduation season, I found myself angry and hurt. My friends with kids the same age were talking about how proud they were of their kids for getting a 4.0, graduating in the top 10 percent of their classes, etc. And here I had all of these wonderful plans for him—my dreams of him getting a good GPA, going to prom (which he actually did), and graduating, proudly walking across the stage. I was almost devastated that it didn't work out. Then I realized those were *my* hopes and dreams.

He's eighteen now, and he's been making these decisions about his future for several years. He is a great learner and can tell you anything you want to know about the *Titanic*. He has always been able to have adult conversations with others, even though he was a child. We told him and told him that if he didn't do his work, he wouldn't graduate on time. And this is the path he chose. We wanted him to be better than we were, too. For some reason, he has chosen to do things the hard way. And then we understood: Even though we did well in school, he is just like my husband and me. We both made bad decisions, especially in our younger adult years.

When our son said he felt like a failure, we told him that not doing well in school doesn't make him a failure in life. He's only eighteen! He is a kind, considerate, loving, caring, sweet, and compassionate young man, and I'm not sure you can actually "teach" that. He's not perfect, but neither are we. I think it's important to remember that we have to trust God to mold him into who He wants Noah to be. Not who we want him to be. Tough lessons for Mom and Dad!

CHAPTER 7

AM I A *Failure?*

*I*f we're honest with ourselves we'll likely admit that some of the questions children ask are the ones we adults are still asking ourselves. "Am I a failure?" is one of those questions that pops into the adult mind on occasion. It's a core question of identity we all face.

In a culture tainted by the Perfection Infection, this question carries even more weight. *If I'm not perfect, I just might be a failure,* one could easily conclude if only looking at extremes. However, extremes aren't where real life takes place. The middle ground of grace is where we need to plant ourselves and our kids. After all, progress is the goal. It's not at all about being perfect but it is about being perfected by the God who has a plan for our lives.

CHANGE THE ADJECTIVE TO A VERB

If you've ever had the opportunity to use a potter's wheel, you know that the initial lump of clay looks completely different after you've turned, pushed, cut away, molded, squeezed, moistened, and shaped. The clay pot you end up with went through quite the process to become something usable. We, too, are like clay on a potter's wheel. In fact the Bible reminds us, "You . . . are our Father. We are the clay, you are the potter; we are all the work of your hand" (Isaiah 64:8). This truth applies to us, and it most definitely applies to our children.

Our children are in process, and the more often we remind ourselves of this, the more grace and love we'll have for them along the way. Just like when they learned to walk, they will stumble, trip, fall down, stand back up, and try once again. They will learn, forget, experience fear, find courage, and take risks in the "becoming" process. They will not be perfect, but they are being perfected.

When the adjective *perfect* (**per**-fikt) changes to the verb *perfect* (per-**fekt**), there's more than just a change of the emphasis from the first syllable to the second, there's also a change of definition. The adjective "perfect" means ideal or without flaws; however, the verb "perfect" means "to improve."[20] A potter who is shaping clay into a pot is "improving" the clay so it can be used in some way. Maybe it will be a pitcher, a bowl, or a vase. God is "improving" each of us every day so we can be used in some way, too. If you can remember that truth when your kids make mistakes, it will help our kids know they're being perfected, but they are in no way failures.

· · · · · · · ·

IS IT SAFE TO MAKE A MISTAKE AT YOUR HOUSE?

One of my favorite Hearts at Home speakers is Dr. Kevin Leman. He's a straight-shootin' kind of guy who says what he thinks. During a keynote message he was talking about the reality of living with the mistakes of our kids. He said, "When your kid spills a drink, he doesn't need a lecture, he needs a rag." I love that simple statement because it reminds me, in a lighthearted way, to stay calm and practical even in the midst of the chaos of having children in the home.

Here's a case in point: Something similar happened in my home while I was writing this chapter. I was wiping off the dining room table after a meal when I discovered a large amount of purple ink at one seat. I said, "Oh my goodness, what is this?" Mark thought it looked like purple marker. I said, "Yes, it does, but who uses purple marker around here?"

At this point my sixteen-year-old — MY SIXTEEN-YEAR-OLD!!! — said, "Well, I sat there when I made Dad's birthday card. I guess the purple marker seeped through the paper. I'm sorry, Mom." I handed the boy a Mr. Clean Magic Eraser, which unfortunately didn't remove the marker. We all laughed and said, "Well, I guess that time will just have to do its work."

I confess that it's not always been that easy to make a mistake at the Savage house. I've come to understand the importance of grace in recent years. If I can spare you and your children any pain, let me encourage you to learn to give grace in the place of anger sooner rather than later. Don't make a mountain out of a molehill. Resist the urge to let your emotions overtake the situation. Exhibit self-control, and

········

respond with something like, "It's okay. We all make mistakes." And if your emotions win on occasion, clean up the relational hurt with, "I'm so sorry for losing my temper. Will you please forgive me?"

If we're all in process, we'll all make mistakes. If we make mistakes, we'll all experience some feelings of failure. However, if we live in an environment where it's safe to make mistakes, we're far less likely to conclude that, by making mistakes, we *are* failures. Progress, not perfection. Mistakes, not failure.

ACCEPT YOURSELF AND YOUR PAST

Before we dig into the "Am I a Failure?" question kids ask, let's push the pause button and understand how our own upbringing affects how we live and how we parent our children today. Whether we think we were raised well or not, it's common to re-create some of our childhood experiences in our homes today. Sometimes we do it intentionally, and sometimes it just naturally happens.

Mark and I like to call the first eighteen years of our lives, when we were still young and living with our parents, our "home internship." This is where we learned about communication, conflict, God, work, responsibility, anger, grace, relationships, and more. When we got married and evaluated our home internships, we discovered that, for some areas of our life together, our home internships served us well. In other areas of our life, however, we decided we needed to undertake a new internship. For instance, in Mark's home internship, he developed a strong work ethic, which has been a huge blessing to our life together. But in Mark's home internship, conflict was handled primarily with rage. Because of that, he discovered he needed to do a new internship in conflict resolution. I needed a new internship in conflict resolution myself, since my home internship led me to sweep conflict under the rug rather than deal with conflict in a healthy way. Our new internship consisted of reading books about healthy conflict resolution, seeing a Christian counselor, and asking friends for accountability as we pursued a new internship.

None of us was raised perfectly, but in most cases our parents did as well as they could considering who they were and what they knew. Most parents are not intentionally bad. Looking back to see if there's anything we need to forgive our parents and ourselves for is wise. Looking back to understand what we've carried forward is wise. Looking back to judge doesn't do anyone any good.

If you were raised by perfectionistic parents, you may be exceptionally hard on yourself because you want to be perfect in many ways, including your parenting. You also may pass the Perfection Infection on to your kids. When reading chapter 2, if you answered yes to many of the questions about the negative effects of perfectionism, this explains why you are more likely challenged to handle your kids' mistakes

Most parents are not intentionally bad.

consistently well. You may think of yourself as a failure (you're not), and your kids may think they're failures (they're not). It doesn't mean you can't grow, and it doesn't mean your kids won't be okay. Accountability with people you trust can help you break habits.

Honestly, to decrease your negative influence, you may need to get very intentional about creating a safe environment for mistakes. There's more you can read for healing and insight, starting with the Bible. Some parents find counseling or a life coach helps tremendously.

. . . .

Accountability with people you trust for changes you want to make can help you break habits. Prayer for guidance and strength is empowering. Our own will to parent differently only goes so far. Sometimes we have to get serious about the new internships we need to pursue. This not only benefits you personally, but it can positively impact your family for generations to come.

WHY DO KIDS MAKE MISTAKES?

We know our kids aren't failures. They can fail a quiz here and there, not win a tournament, and not earn a raise during their first job review, but none of that makes them failures. They will make mistakes, though. They're human!

To best help our kids overcome their mistakes and not feel like failures, we need to know why they make them. We need to listen closely and observe intently for causes so we know how to support them. Let's explore eight reasons kids make mistakes.

1. They need more experience.

When kids complain that school is hard, remind them that if it were easy, they wouldn't need to go. School—and much of life—is about trying new things. We must let our kids know they're not stupid when they get things wrong. If they believe this too long, they'll not only stop trying, they'll stop dreaming about and believing in their future. Mistakes are a part of life, and they often show up when we need more experience.

2. They need to be taught in order to be successful.

Mistakes can occur when content and tasks are new and teaching hasn't yet occurred. Kids might enjoy trying things on their own, but then can get very frustrated when their independent approach doesn't go well. This is common when younger kids try to do what their older siblings can do. Protect their self-esteem when you notice that the reason they did something wrong was simply because they need help or more instruction.

3. They need more time to learn something.

Errors occur because kids didn't learn something well enough, although teaching has begun. These mistakes are a part of learning. They happen, and it's no one's fault. It's not that your child intentionally chose to be wrong. It's not that the adult who taught them explained things poorly. Don't quickly assume blame when your kids make mistakes. That's not healthy for you or them. Kids learn by doing and experimenting.

We're the same way. How did you learn to drive? By driving imperfectly for a while. How did you decide which barbeque sauce you prefer? By cooking with one and then another. Did you make a mistake? No. It was a "learn by doing" experience, not a "mistake by doing" experience. The language we use to discuss mistakes matters; this includes what we say to our kids and what we say inside our heads when thinking about them.

4. They need healthy motivation to do things well.

Sometimes kids make mistakes because they don't want the additional pressure that comes with excellence. Maybe your son's teacher keeps calling on him because he's always attentive and right, but your son wants to take a break from that. Maybe peers have teased your daughter for being "teacher's pet." Maybe your oldest is feeling like all your happiness is on his shoulders. That's unhealthy motivation and creates a lot of pressure for any child.

5. They need our understanding and attention.

Kids will occasionally fail at something or make mistakes just to push our buttons. Let's face it: They are smart little people even at a young age, and they learn the power of manipulation early. Sometimes they take out their anger toward us by not doing well something they know is important to us. In these cases, responding with understanding is important. When the time is right, and depending on their age, let them know you understand they're angry or frustrated. But also help your children see they're making unwise decisions and you'd rather have them talk with you about their feelings.

6. They need more modeling and instruction related to character and obedience.

Sometimes mistakes are an issue of character. Kids might hurry through a task or assignment so they can get back to their video games. They can choose to not double-check their work because pride is in their way and they're just convinced they haven't made any mistakes. They can become impatient with themselves or others and stop working on chores

....

and assignments. As parents, we need to discern whether our children are making occasional errors in judgment or if they've developed consistent character flaws that need to be addressed.

7. They need self-respect, self-control, and respect for others modeled for them and taught to them.

Sometimes kids' strengths get them into trouble. Too much of a good thing is not a good thing! For example, word-smart kids might talk too much. Logic-smart kids with a heightened curiosity may ask questions to keep you distracted and to extend bedtime. Picture-smart kids may draw on a report you left on the table, and kids with musical strengths may drum with their fingers or pencils until you can't handle it anymore. We don't want to paralyze their strengths by overreacting and being too critical, but we do need to teach the concepts of self-control and respecting others.

8. They need sleep, food, and/or emotional stability.

Do you sometimes underperform or make unhealthy decisions when you're tired, hungry, or emotionally vulnerable? So do kids. You might discover your daughter should start her homework after having a snack. Your son may not be handling the long day of school well and may need to go to bed thirty minutes earlier than you originally thought. To track patterns, you can keep a written record of their misbehavior using a calendar or a list. After recording a few days of when mistakes and misbehavior occur, who was present, if it was near mealtime, or if they were fatigued, you can often identify possible strategies to decrease the misbehavior.

· · · · · · · ·

It's okay, in the midst of mistakes, to verbalize that our children are not failing or failures. Look for impressionable moments when kids need the reassurance that making mistakes is how people learn. You may not be happy with their choices, and discipline may be necessary, but also let them know they're not stupid. Letting our kids know they're not mistakes even when they make mistakes is always important. It's probably most important to communicate this when we're frustrated. This reassures them even in the tough moments of life.

HOW CAN WE ENCOURAGE OUR KIDS?

Establishing a culture of encouragement in our homes is essential. When we en*courage* kids, we give them courage. It's empowering, freeing, and strengthening. When encouragement is the norm, children will learn they can take risks, try new things, ask for help, and make mistakes without the fear of losing the acceptance, love, and support of their parents.

Encouragement will empower, free, and strengthen you, too. It's what will help you be compassionate and consistent. Courage will enable you to love your kids even on the days they disappoint you. Courage will also give you the strength to disappoint them with policies and consequences earned by their choices.

I have every confidence that you want an encouraging culture in your home, but I also know that's not always easy. We get down on ourselves when we see our weaknesses in our kids, yell when we know it's not best, and don't have the energy to do laundry for the fourth day in a row. Then our daughter spills her milk, our son comes in from the backyard filthy, and they pick at each other all night.

. . . .

Life isn't easy. Fatigue is normal. Frustration is, too. Learning not to act unkindly in our frustration is a journey requiring grace for ourselves and our kids. There are, however, steps we can take to increase encouragement in our home. Pick one or two of these eleven Encouragement Enhancers to focus on over the next few weeks:

1. *Don't expect perfection.* When we expect perfection, we notice every little thing that's wrong and that creates an environment of discouragement.
2. *Encourage childlike behavior.* There's a difference between childish behavior and age-appropriate childlike behavior. Discourage the first and encourage the second.
3. *Value what your kids learn.* We need to pay at least as much attention to what's being learned as we do to grades being earned and performances at games and concerts. This is one way we communicate that our kids are more than what they do and how they do.
4. *Be optimistic.* We choose optimism when helping kids study and practice and when asking about their days. Like all other aspects of parenting, optimism is a choice. It doesn't mean we expect perfection. Optimism is taking the most hopeful or cheerful view and expecting the best outcomes.
5. *Resist the urge to judge all performances.* Even though our kids expect to be critiqued, we don't judge or grade everything. Our past behavior, teachers and coaches, the games/apps kids play, and competition television shows have already taught kids to expect someone to tell them how they've done. One way to emphasize

learning rather than performance is not always to ask about their scores or grades.

6. *Ask them how they feel.* When talking about one of their athletic competitions, concerts, or tests, sometimes ask first how satisfied they were with the outcome. If they earned a 95 percent when they wanted a 100 percent, our praise will fall on deaf ears. If they earn an 83 percent and are grateful that score is not worse because the test was more difficult than expected, our displeasure will discourage them. Two-way conversations about grades, concerts, and competitions will be more profitable than one-way judgments.

7. *Notice their strengths.* Point out their character, attitude, and action strengths so they'll use them to compensate for weaknesses and to help them when they work to make progress in weak areas.

8. *Don't worry about their challenges.* Understand some areas will remain challenges for our kids no matter how hard they try. Resist the temptation to worry, realizing you have weaknesses, too, and they've not held you back as much as your parents probably worried they would. Trying to get kids to change what they can't improve is a sure way to discourage them. If necessary, we need to change our hopes and expectations for them. We haven't failed, and neither have they. Different isn't bad. It's just different.

9. *Celebrate what's real.* When one child deserves to be celebrated for something significant (e.g., no Cs on a report card for the first time in a year, a soccer championship, art being displayed in the county library), don't create fake celebrations for our other kids in order to be "fair." Use these opportunities to teach children

to genuinely appreciate their siblings, their talents, and their choice to develop and use them well.

10. *Introduce them to overcomers.* Discuss relatives and local people your kids know who have overcome great odds to be joyful and successful. Read biographies and autobiographies of people who have been highly successful even though they also struggled. You can use Bible heroes like David, Paul, Peter, and Moses to make this point, too. These people can help you convince your kids that perfection should not be their expectation or goal but that learning from their mistakes makes a better expectation or goal. We all can learn our greatest lessons from our greatest challenges. It's our choice.

> *Look forward with hope and an expectation that God will help you if you ask.*

11. *Have fun together.* Play with your kids. Don't plan every last minute of the week's schedule, so you'll have breathing room to say yes more often to their requests to do things with you. Relationships are deepened while building forts and having tea parties with your little ones and going shopping and watching ball games with your older ones. The fun, relaxed moments you share make tough times easier to walk through and go a long way to creating an encouraging family culture.

Be patient with yourself as you work to improve the encouraging environment in your family. If you choose too many things to change, you and your kids will be overwhelmed and little progress will be made. Don't look back with shame or guilt. Look forward with hope and an expectation that God will help you if you ask. The Bible tells us that,

....

"The things that are impossible with people are possible with God" (Luke 18:27 NASB).

WHAT ABOUT THE BIG STUFF?

As the CEO, I lead the Executive Team at Hearts at Home. The women on my team are fellow moms in the same season of mothering I'm in, which means we're all parenting teenagers and/or young adults. As we sit down for our weekly meetings, many times I start with, "So how's everything at home? Anyone arrested? Suspended from school? Any discoveries since we last met?" I ask the question somewhat humorously, but we all appreciate having a place to be open and honest about whatever it is we are dealing with at home — no judgment, no shame, just real life. Every one of us on that team has dealt with some big stuff with our kids.

If you have teenagers or young adults, you just might be relieved to read that. It feels good to be reassured you're not the only one. When your kids are little, parenting is physically exhausting. When your kids get older, parenting is emotionally and mentally exhausting. Their problems get bigger. The stakes get higher. The mistakes can have bigger consequences. Accepting each child for who they are takes on a new level of meaning.

If you still have little ones, don't freak out as you read about the possible challenges ahead. Thank God for the season of parenting you're in and for learning about leaving behind Perfection Infection parenting at this stage of the game. It will serve you well someday when you face bigger issues with your kids. You don't need to be weighed down

· · · · · · · ·

worrying about what others will think as you're trying to help your children when their future's at stake.

Good parenting doesn't provide any surety your kids will make good choices. That's true when your toddler throws a fit at the zoo, and it's also true when your son becomes a father at age sixteen. You're not a failure if either of those things happen, and neither is your child. Good parenting doesn't guarantee your child will not have emotional or mental health issues. Sometimes our kids are affected by genetics, sometimes they are influenced by culture, and sometimes they just plain old struggle simply because they do.

No parent wants to hear these words, but some of us have or will:

"I got kicked out of school today."

"I'm pregnant."

"My girlfriend is pregnant."

"I think I'm gay."

"I'm in jail."

"I flunked out of school and lost my scholarships."

No parent wants to hear someone say this about our child, but some of us have or will:

"Your child has schizophrenia. He'll live with this the rest of his life."

"Your child has an eating disorder. She needs residential treatment."

"Your child was caught shoplifting from our theme park."

"I caught your child cheating on an exam."

"Your child has severe clinical depression. This was a suicide
attempt."

"Your adopted child has reactive attachment disorder. He's deeply
wounded from his past."

No parent wants to say these words to his or her child, but many of
us will or have:

"What are those marks on your arm? Are you cutting yourself?"

"Would you like to explain this bong that I found in your bedroom?"

"What is this bottle of alcohol doing in the back of your closet?"

"You told me you spent the night at your friend's house last night,
but her mother said you weren't there."

"What are these pills I found in your car?"

"Can you explain these magazines I found under your mattress?"

If you have found yourself hearing or saying any of these statements
or something like them, stop and remind yourself of the truth. Your
child is not a failure. You are not a failure as a parent. Life happens.
Choices are made. Diagnoses are given. Discoveries occur.

And God is bigger than it all.

These situations can either tear you apart as a parent, or they can
make you stronger. They can rip a marriage in two or bind you together. If you're knee-deep in Perfection Infection parenting, worried
about what others will think and how this looks, you'll likely be torn
apart by these difficult circumstances. However, if you've successfully
left Perfection Infection parenting behind and have made progress in

loving your kids for who they are, you'll find these situations will make you stronger. You'll take compassion to a new level, perceive more acutely, accept more intently, and love more deeply than ever before. You may not know this, but Jesus' earthly family tree included adulterers, murderers, prostitutes, liars, and more. Heartbreak is not lost on God. He understands mistakes, and He can do some of His best work through the cracks in our lives and the cracks in our children's lives.

Your child's choices and/or diagnoses do not define you. Your child's choices and/or diagnoses do not define him or her. Sometimes imperfection becomes very obvious, and when it does it's important to keep a godly perspective. Even in the toughest situations of life, no matter the cause, God will give you what you need. You'll be able to say, as my friend Jennifer Rothschild says, "It is not well with my circumstances, but it is well with my soul."

In difficult parenting situations, I have found strength and hope in Psalm 34:18, which says, "The Lord is close to the brokenhearted and saves those who are crushed in spirit." I really like the way *The Message* puts that verse: "If your heart is broken, you'll find God right there; if you're kicked in the gut, he'll help you catch your breath." Let's face it: there are times when we're parenting imperfect children that we will feel kicked in the gut. It's then, more than ever, that our kids need to know we really love them for who they are.

APPLY THE ANTIDOTES

As our kids learn to process—and even appreciate—mistakes, it's even more important that we apply the Perfection Infection antidotes liberally. These life-giving responses from us give them the courage to carry on even when things are tough. Give large doses of . . .

Compassion

When kids make mistakes, they want to know someone cares. They also want to know they're not alone. If you can share a time with them when you made a mistake by doing something similar, it will help them believe you understand.

Perception

If you sense your child is getting down on himself—moving from "I made a mistake" to "I'm a failure"—don't hesitate to call out what you sense he may be feeling (or telling himself). Reassure him that mistakes are normal and what's important is that we learn from them.

Acceptance

The more we are accepting of our children, the more accepting they are of themselves. Accept the things that are hard for them and, if needed, help them find ways to fill the gap with their weakness (e.g., if you have a child who has a difficult time with spelling, teach her to type out her status in Microsoft Word before she puts it on Facebook so she can benefit from spell-check). Accepting doesn't mean agreeing with. If you're dealing with a big issue with your child, accepting simply means acknowledging and recognizing the reality of your child's circumstances.

Love

When we love our children in action and in word, regardless of the mistakes they make, they grow to understand what unconditional love looks like. God loves us that way. One way we are all being "perfected" is learning to love more like Him each and every day. Thank God today that you get to learn more about unconditional love through the parenting experience.

AM I A FAILURE?

Encouraging children when they make mistakes or feel like failures is a privilege and important responsibility. When we encourage them, we give them courage so they'll strive to work through and past their challenges. We also help them know that learning from mistakes is an important part of the process of growing up. Even in the hard parts of parenting, let's be encouragers of process so our kids don't equate mistakes with failure!

CHAPTER 8

WHAT'S *My* PURPOSE?

When our kids were little, the tuck-into-bed routine included a story and praying together. When we were teaching them how to pray, we would do a "fill-in-the-blank" prayer that included "God, I praise You because You are _____ (holy, faithful, truth, good, love, etc). God, please forgive me for _____ (hitting my sister, lying to Mom, etc). God, I thank You for _____ (my teacher, my friends, my family, the chance to see Grandma today). God, please help _____ (me, my sister, my friend, Grandma, etc.)." This helped them learn how to talk to God in a way that was more than a shopping list with a give-me-this-and-give-me-that mindset. Had I known then what I know now about casting vision for my kids' purpose in this world, I would have prayed with them and for them about their purpose in this world, too. Teaching by talking to God is a great place to keep what's most important in life at the forefront of your children's hearts and minds.

Every human being longs for significance. Understanding why we're in the world and what impact we can make gives us inherent value both as a member of society and a member of God's family. We all have both general and specific purpose in this world. Let's explore what both of those look like.

GOD'S BIG-PICTURE PURPOSES FOR US

In Psalm 8:3–4, King David addresses purpose when he asks God, "When I consider your heavens, the work of your fingers . . . what is mankind that you are mindful of them, human beings that you care for them?" David is essentially saying, "So God, just why did You bother creating us?" God created human beings to have a relationship with Him and with one another. We need Him; there's a God-shaped void in all of us that we will try to fill with other things unless He is in our hearts. God doesn't force Himself on us, but He extends His hand and asks us to grab it. This happens when we say something like, "God I need You. I need You to be the leader of my life. I'm grateful that You sent Your Son, Jesus, to die in my place. Thank You for Your grace and salvation."

When God is leading our lives, He allows us to be part of His work and His plan so we can learn more about Him and ourselves. In our relationship with God, we have four general purposes.

Purpose 1: To Praise God

Every child conceived was created by a loving and intentional God who knew what He was doing. He had a vision for their lives, and He still does. Talking about God, David, an author of many psalms, put it this way: "For you created my inmost being; you knit me together in my mother's womb. I praise you because I am fearfully and wonderfully made; your works are wonderful, I know that full well" (Psalm 139:13–14). From a young age, kids can learn about being grateful to God for making them. God didn't have to make them, but He wanted to. He created each one uniquely (translated "wonderfully") and He wants us to be in awe of what He did (translated "fearfully").

To easily praise God necessitates a thinking pattern of gratitude. Our children need to hear us thank God for creating them the way He did. (This is what I would have added to our tuck-in prayer if I could go back and do it over again!) We need to model acceptance and even joy over them, down to their hard-to-brush hair, tendency to break into song, unending energy, and insatiable curiosity.

Are we happy about their interest in ballet when we wanted a soccer player, their deep soul-searching nature when we'd rather they process out loud, and their fascination with numbers when we've always been a bit math-phobic? Verbalizing appreciation of those kinds of differences helps us accept our children and helps our children believe they have unique design and purpose. Recognizing their design was chosen for them by a loving God gives our kids an internal strength. This belief can serve as a vaccine against bullying and teasing as they learn to stand up for themselves and appreciate who they are.

....

Purpose 2: To Do Good Works

When God knit each child together the way He wanted to, He gave them abilities and interests. God tells us this in Ephesians 2:10: "For we are God's handiwork, created in Christ Jesus to do good works, which God prepared in advance for us to do." Each and every child was created to do certain things—good things. Our kids' purpose is to do well those things they can do well. When our kids are grateful for the talents they have, it keeps the Perfection Infection at bay because they're focused on what they have, rather than on what they don't have.

It's important to note that we weren't created to do "perfect" works, just "good" works. That word, in the original language used in the Bible, means works of upright character and moral excellence. These would include activities that positively influence others.

Kids need to know their strengths so they can believe in God's handiwork on their behalf. But they also need to believe He can use their weaknesses, too. If you remember, spelling doesn't come easy to Kathy, yet she's written this book and others, blogs regularly, and is well educated. When kids understand they were created by an intentional God and all His handiwork is what lets them do good work, they're less likely to come up with excuses for why they can't be involved in something they don't necessarily do well. If you have older kids who have hesitated to get involved in some aspect of service, what weaknesses seem to be the ones holding them back? Could you cast a vision for them to see even their weaknesses as something God can use or something God can accommodate in some way?

Purpose 3: To Be God's PR Agent

Every one of us was created by God for His glory (Isaiah 43:7). Just what does it mean to bring glory to God? It means we are giving God good PR! We're bringing positive attention to God and representing Him well.

One way we glorify God is when we become who He designed us to be. When we help our kids become and accept who God made them to be, and not who we wish they might be, we glorify Him in our parenting. When we help them fully come into their own, God is pleased and He looks good because His creation is "fearfully and wonderfully made; [His] works are wonderful."

When we rejoice in our kids' interests, God looks good. When we're glad they are who they are, it sends a message to the world around us. When we help them revel in their discoveries, God is glorified. Cheering for their school team when they didn't make it represents God well. Studying diligently to earn a C when a D was a strong possibility is glorifying to God. To help them stop complaining about their thin, limp hair and to stop lusting after their friend's hair glorifies God. Understanding prescribed medicine to affect behavior is a supplement to their own choices, rather than a substitute, gives God glory.

When we rejoice in our kids' interests, God looks good.

Adding glorifying God to the goal of obeying parents is powerful. Now, when they're alone in their bedrooms deciding whether to choose gaming instead of finishing their assigned homework reading, they have additional motivation to choose the book. They have a reason to behave the same at a friend's house as they do at ours. They may choose not to speed even when we're not riding in the car with them.

· · · · · · · ·

Lots of negative feedback can cause kids to believe they can't glorify God. Kids raised thinking they're never good enough because we question every point lost on every paper or test won't believe they can glorify God. If we contact our son's coach every time we don't believe he played enough minutes, he may question his skill and contribution and conclude he can't glorify God. Focusing on the positive aspects of who our children are is not only encouraging but also helps them discover their purpose and embrace bringing God glory with their lives.

Purpose 4: To Leave the World a Better Place

One of Kathy's favorite ways of talking with kids about the beautiful reality that they're created on purpose with purpose is to challenge them to live long enough to leave the world a better place. Just think about it: Our older kids have seen our broken world on numerous websites, YouTube videos, and twenty-four-hour raw, unedited news footage. For all ages, there are also the up close and personal challenges of family dysfunction, peer-group bullying, disappointed parents, and fears about the future. Kids can be overwhelmed and think there's nothing they can do.

We can help our kids understand that they don't have to grow up in order to become difference makers. They are created to do good works now. Many young kids today have raised money to build schools in Uganda or dig water wells in Kenya, find the cure for cancer, and build new front steps for their grandparents' house. When they reach out in friendship to a new kid in the youth group, help you with their younger sister, and write Daddy a love note to slip into his suitcase before he leaves on his next business trip, they're also making the world a better place.

....

Children who try to be perfect to keep us happy are less likely to believe they can be difference makers. Perhaps this is the extra motivation you need to make sure you are accepting your kids for who they are. When we don't, they can become more self-centered and less likely to think about blessing others.

Kids need to be serving when they're young. They don't have to wait to grow up. When Anne was a toddler, I served as a Meals on Wheels volunteer and I brought Anne along on my weekly route. This was a great opportunity for her to become comfortable with older people and to bring a smile to their faces even as a young child. As our family grew, we volunteered to do the church service at our local nursing home. Anne and Erica led singing while Evan played the piano. Austin was just a preschooler, so his job was to pass out hymnals and hugs. The older people loved getting to interact with the kids. When tornadoes hit Joplin, Missouri, Mark and I took Austin and Kolya to volunteer with cleanup and rebuilding. The boys worked hard in the summer heat. They experienced what it feels like to make the world a better place and for God to use you to do His work.

Watch for opportunities to introduce your kids to serving others. This gives them purpose and allows them to impact their world in some way. Jesus gave His life for us. He modeled what it's like to serve others in a sacrificial way. The more we give our kids the opportunity to experience God's big-picture purposes, the better off they are in understanding their purpose to praise God, do good works, bring Him glory, and make the world a better place.

HOW DO WE HELP OUR KIDS BELIEVE THEY HAVE UNIQUE PURPOSE?

Purpose is discovered by influence and experience. I can see that in my own life. When I was a freshman in high school, I was hired by Florence, a woman in our church, to stay with her mentally handicapped adult daughter, Barbie. Florence competed in tennis tournaments all over the United States so I would stay with Barbie in her absence. Although at first I stayed with Barbie during daytime hours, eventually Florence began to ask me to do overnight care. That was a lot of responsibility for a young lady who couldn't yet drive. However, Florence's influence indicated I was capable. My experience in caring for her daughter over the years helped me discover that I could make a difference in someone's life. Although Florence is no longer alive, I still connect with Barbie when I'm back in Avon, Indiana. She loves to tell me about her activities, her animals, and all her aches and pains. Even in her limited mental capacity, Barbie blesses me. Caring for her in my early years gave me purpose.

In another instance around that same time, my father asked me to fill in as an occasional summer receptionist at the school district administrative offices where he worked. I was probably sixteen and in charge of a good-sized switchboard. My dad's belief that I could handle the job told me I was responsible. The experience gave me purpose.

Those opportunities, together with others that were afforded me in my growing-up years, planted seeds of purpose in me as a leader. I am grateful for the influence and experience that helped shape me into the person I am today.

How do we help our kids believe they have purpose? In addition

....

to providing them influence and experience, they also need hope for today and for tomorrow. Present-day and future-day hope is essential for kids to believe they have purpose. They must not see their situation as hopeless or the world so lost they can't imagine helping in some way. They need to know they can make a difference. They must understand they have present value and future potential.

Our son Austin has a tender heart. When his older brother and sister traveled to Jamaica on a youth group mission trip, nine-year-old Austin announced that he wanted to do a sword-throwing show to raise money for the mission team's work projects. Every day he took his plastic toy swords out in the yard and worked up a routine to music. Soon he wanted to print up invitations to give to people at church to come to his show. I couldn't imagine this endeavor would be successful, and every part of me wanted to discourage Austin in this "foolish" event. I refrained, however, realizing I needed to be a dream-maker, not a dream-taker. I needed to put aside my fear of his failure and influence his belief he had purpose. Believe it or not, fifteen people came to his show and between the ticket price and donations accepted at the door, he earned more than $100 for the special project! Our kids can make a difference; sometimes we just have to get out of the way!

We can also help our kids find purpose by leading them to people they can serve. When our kids get their eyes off themselves, find others to build up, and see themselves making a positive difference, they'll believe they can leave the world a better place.

Your family can serve people together, like we did with the church service at the nursing home. One family I know chooses to serve Thanksgiving dinner together at a local homeless shelter. Another family serves an elderly woman in their church whenever she needs help caring for her house and yard. While it's certainly about helping others, it's also a great way to unify the family and help siblings work together as a team. Because you're with them, you can provide specific feedback to encourage them. They'll believe they can make a difference because they already are. This can motivate them to learn key truths, develop character, grow in their faith, develop more skills, and grow in joy.

Continue to give direction and encouragement, resisting the urge to lead them in the direction you want them to go.

We can also help our kids find purpose by giving them direction. This is especially true for two kinds of kids: those who don't know or believe in their talents and those who are multitalented and multi-passionate. Our kids who don't know their talents need to see ways to use the skills and interests they do have, even if they're not as strong as others. For example, older elementary kids who don't read perfectly probably still read well enough to volunteer to read to kindergartners. Directing them to step up to help the little ones can build their confidence. Preteens and teens who aren't coordinated enough to make their school soccer team can help with a team of young children. Kids who think they don't draw with expertise can draw well enough to make cards to encourage people in a nursing home or soldiers overseas. Creating opportunities for them, whatever skills and interests they have, will demonstrate they're not broken and they don't have to be perfect to have purpose.

The second group of kids needing our direction is the multi-talented, multi-passionate older ones afraid to make decisions for fear they won't choose what's best. In these cases, there's often not a wrong answer to how to fulfill purpose. They need our help and direction to courageously choose something. Of course, it's fine for children to graduate from high school and have absolutely no idea what they want to do with their life. That's normal! Just continue to give them direction and encouragement to explore and discover, resisting the urge to lead them in the direction you want them to go. Consider asking questions like:

What do you feel you do well?

What brings you joy?

What fulfills you?

What intrigues you?

What kind of problems do you try to solve or figure out?

What do you dream of doing or becoming?

What do you get excited about?

Kathy recently met with a college student ready to begin his senior year. He was on academic probation for the second time and had lost his financial aid. He told Kathy and his dad that none of his courses interested him and he wasn't sure about his major anymore or what he wanted to do when graduating. She asked him, "What concerns you? What's wrong in the world that you'd like to speak into?" After a while, he opened up and they talked about relating what he would be learning his senior year to those issues. His demeanor changed. Later that day, he and his dad had a long, positive conversation about his future. That conversation seemed to be just the direction he needed to move from indifference to purpose.

Another way we can aid our kids in finding purpose is to help them "find five." This exercise can be done as a family and will result in each

· · · · · · · ·

person identifying five things to be, do, have, and help. Even when we know our kids well, we don't always know everything that interests them in the moment. They may keep some of it private, and they may change their minds often as they're influenced by what's going on around them and the people they interact with. It's valuable for us to participate because it helps our kids know what's on our hearts and minds. They need to understand that even as adults, we continue to have hopes and dreams.

The exercise is simple. Give everyone in the family a piece of paper. Have them fold it twice to create four boxes and open it back up. In one, write the word *be*. In the others, write *do, have,* and *help*. Now, taking adequate time, have each person write five things they want to be, do, have, and help in their lifetime. Young kids can dictate their ideas to an older sibling or parent who writes their ideas down for them.

The answers can be telling. For instance, if everyone struggles to think of groups of people or causes to help, it may indicate you don't talk a lot in your family about serving. If thinking of five things to have is easiest, that may indicate materialism is an issue or kids are used to getting things they ask for. You can look to see if the "be" and "do" categories line up well or not. For instance, does your daughter list *mommy* but not *wife*? If so, you might want to help her see the importance of doing things in a better order.

Another beneficial way to use this exercise is to create a family mission statement. If your kids are old enough, you can involve them. Think and pray about the ideal five things in each category. What do you want them to **be**? Content, growing followers of Christ, joyful, teachable? What do you want them to **do** in their lifetime? Serve, give,

....

grow? What do you want them to **have**? A healthy marriage or confidence if single? A meaningful purpose? Enjoyable friendships? And what about **helping**? Family members, orphans, the poor. What cause compels you? A family mission statement can help you keep your priorities in focus as you decide how to spend time together as a family and what conversations to have regularly. It also models having a vision for purpose. Putting that vision on paper makes it tangible and prioritized.

It's common for kids not to know their purpose; that's why it's important that we assist them in discovering it. Honestly, it's common for adults to sometimes not have a sense of purpose, too. If that's you, you can explore right along with your kids. After all, it's never too late for any of us to have a vision for how we can impact our world! Explore along with your kids. It's never too late to impact our world!

In understanding purpose, it's important for us to be aware of how technology in our culture affects purpose. The digital age has made finding purpose easier in some ways. Yet it also complicates the search for purpose in other ways. Let's explore both of those realities.

TECHNOLOGY AND PURPOSE

Kids' use of digital toys and tools influences them in many ways, including whether they believe they have purpose and what that purpose might be. From a positive perspective, computers, the Internet, social networking, mobile phones, gaming, television, cable, movies, iPods, and digital cameras and cameras on phones have been incredibly influential in opening up our children's minds to possibilities. Technology has made our world smaller and more tangible with websites, twenty-four-hour news, YouTube videos, and the like providing information

....

about people groups to serve and causes to embrace. These sources also report on people, including children, teens, and young adults who are making a positive difference. These stories empower our kids to believe they too can make a difference. Be aware, though, that they can also cause our child great pressure to figure out what they can do. If they compare, or if they hear us comparing, they may feel inadequate and without realizing it, the Perfection Infection can raise its ugly head.

We can temper that extreme with encouragement that we can all make a difference in some way. It doesn't matter if our influence reaches hundreds of people, like building a well in Africa might, or if we make a difference in the life of our neighbor who needed the sticks picked up in her yard after a storm. Both are equally important. They allow our children to love and care for others in Jesus' name.

Through the Internet, our youngest, Austin, became familiar with a ministry called Come&Live.[21] As a musician, Austin was drawn to their mission of sharing musical art royalty-free in an effort to direct profits to meet global needs like poverty, human trafficking, homelessness, widows and orphans in distress, victims of war, and many others who legitimately need help. When Austin got his first job at the age of fifteen, he decided to give a monthly donation to the Come&Live ministry. This opportunity came about through technology, and it is one way Austin has identified a passion and a purpose.

Kids who spend hours in front of video games and technology run the risk of operating under an erroneous view of their place in the world. If you have a "gamer" or a kid drawn to technology, it's important to set healthy limits of time spent on technology. That too was our Austin. He would have played video games for hours, days, and even

. . . .

weeks if we hadn't set boundaries and limits. A simple kitchen timer did the trick. When Austin was younger, we only allowed two hours of gaming a day in the summer (and not consecutive hours. He could do two one-hour sessions, four thirty-minute time frames, or however he wanted to split it up). We required him to start the timer before he started playing. If I found him playing without the timer set, he lost his privilege immediately for the rest of that day. As he grew older and had friends over to play video games, we changed the boundaries to one hour on, then two hours off. Again, the timer was used to empower him to self-manage his balance boundaries. During the school year, gaming was limited to thirty minutes a day on school days, and two days per week were set aside as "no screen" days.

Whether it's technology or something else our kids get obsessed with, it's important that we help them set boundaries for balance in their lives. Be prepared for the pushback. After all, your child will think you're the only mean parent who makes her kids stop playing video games. Stay strong, though, because you are helping them with the life skill of balance that will serve them well throughout their adult years.

What technology triggers exist when kids spend too much time in the digital world? There are three risks they face over time. First, they may get used to the incorrect idea that they must be entertained. As a result, they may only want to participate in fast-paced, challenging, and entertaining activities (which immediately rules out much of school!). They may complain about boredom and quickly decide they're bored. They may believe job tasks should be entertaining, which we know isn't true for the career world. They may also complain about some teachers and homework. Kids who believe they need to be entertained in this world may not persevere with chores at home because they're boring, routine, and not challenging.

A second risk that too much technology may introduce is the quest for happiness. A lot of video game story lines teach that happiness is a right. The goal is to win, achieve, or get more coins. The result is a sense of happiness, however virtual or fleeting, that can be addictive. As adults, we know happiness isn't always the end result of things we have to do. In fact, much of our purpose in this world is to serve others. Technology is about serving ourselves. This can be another reason a child exposed to large doses of technology struggles to persevere with people or tasks that don't register on their happiness meter.

Expand your child's ability to dream and imagine whenever possible.

Technology also teaches our kids everything should be easy. Writing is made easier because of functions like copy-and-paste and spell-check on the computer. Our DVR makes it simple to copy television shows for watching later. iPods allow us to have music with us at all times. We can auto-correct and crop pictures. When something stops working, we can turn it off and turn it back on. Miraculously, many things fix themselves. Because of this, our children run the risk of not understanding the value of hard work. They may be satisfied with the status quo rather than eager to learn new skills and talents. Their short-term, look-for-the-easy-way-out perspective will blind them to valuable opportunities to discover purpose.

Technology is here to stay. It's certainly valuable and has made our lives much easier in many ways. How can a parent combat the technology triggers that don't serve our children well in finding purpose in the world? Here are four strategies to consider:

· · · · · · · ·

Teach your child how to cope with boredom, not escape it.

When he wants to escape boredom, his goal is wrong. Boredom is a fact of life, so he must learn how to handle it well. Because the desire to avoid boredom will influence his decisions, we don't want him to miss out on opportunities to change the world. Help kids cope with boredom, not escape it.

You and your child can make a list of about thirty things he can do when he is bored. Number the choices, and post it where he can see it. When he's bored, he can look at the list to be reminded of something he can do. If he complains to you, you can say, "Go choose #5, 17, or 28."

Another way to cope with boredom is to choose to be satisfied imagining, wondering, and daydreaming. Our own thoughts can be entertaining, but sometimes those thoughts need to be nurtured. Head outside with your child and a blanket on a sunny summer day to lie on your backs and look at clouds. Share what things you each "see" in the clouds. You can also do this same exercise while driving somewhere and looking at the clouds through the car window. While it's easy to plop our kids in front of technology to keep them busy, expand your child's ability to dream and imagine whenever possible. Mark and I recently did this with our three-year-old granddaughter while making a one-hour drive. It was amazing the things her three-year-old mind saw in the clouds!

Let your child know his brain is wired for engagement.

It's not entertainment he needs; it's tasks and ideas to stimulate thoughts and feelings. Our goal should not be to keep our kids entertained. That's pressure we don't need. Engagement is more appropriate. One

. . . .

example of this is to hand your older child a map when you are driving somewhere. Let her follow the route with her finger. Ask her to identify cities and states that are north, south, east, and west of where you are. In the day and age of GPS units, talking phones, and Mapquest, this kind of activity establishes spatial context and big-picture thinking that helps kids engage in their world. Help kids choose engagement rather than entertainment for their minds.

Model and talk actively about joy and fulfillment being more important than happiness.

Explain that always being happy isn't realistic, but being consistently joyful is. Happiness is an emotion usually caused by external factors like favorite foods, fun activities, or unexpected gifts. Joy is an emotion caused by internal contentment. Happiness is momentary. Joy is everlasting. While happiness appears and disappears, joy is consistent because it's based upon a godly perspective in our lives. The more you grasp joy in your heart, the more your kids will learn that joy can remain even when life's circumstances are hard. Help kids value joy and fulfillment more than happiness.

Model and teach character attributes like perseverance and diligence.

It's okay for your children to see you experience frustration, but it's equally important they see you persevere in the midst of that frustration. This shows them how to be overcomers. It reminds children that they can use their strengths to compensate for weaknesses when pursuing mission and purpose in life.

. . . .

You can also share times from your life when you've stretched yourself and been willing to work hard. Talk about how fulfilling it was. When my youngest was small, he would say, "Tell me a story from your life, Mom," as I tucked him in bed. This became a great opportunity for me to share some of the experiences I had that taught me life lessons of purpose, diligence, and perseverance. Your child doesn't have to ask you to share those stories, you can start doing that on your own. Your vulnerability may be the best teacher for helping your child catch the vision of how to find purpose in this world. These kinds of conversations also counterbalance the lack of relational connection found in digital technology.

Make in-person relationships a priority.

Facebook has not only shifted the word *friend* from being a noun to being a verb, it's also given new meaning to the concept of friendship. Because we can be so connected to others through social media, we're less likely to really invest in face-to-face, real-life relationships. Because of this trend, we need to seek a balance in how much time our kids spend with "friends" online and how much time they spend actually being with people. Prioritizing in-person relationships will make a difference in your child's future marriage and in his or her ability to carry on conversation, handle conflict, and care about others.

In-person relationships might be something to evaluate in your own life, too. Do your kids see you spend time with friends? Do they observe you making people a priority over technology? Our own habits influence our kids' habits, so if we want to change their habits, sometimes we have to start with our own!

········

APPLYING THE ANTIDOTES

As children come to understand their purpose in this world, they will have highs and lows in the process. There will be mountaintop experiences and seasons when they feel they are in a pit of frustration and hopelessness. All across the spectrum of experiences, it's important we apply the antidotes to help our kids stay healthy in their perspective and resist the infection of perfection in their lives.

Compassion

Compassion is extremely important in handling times when our kids experience frustration, disappointment, and worry as they try to figure out this world and their purpose in it. Resist the urge to give a pick-yourself-up-by-the-bootstraps lecture and listen instead. Really listen to their heart cries. Where are they hurting? Are they worried or struggling? Respond with empathetic statements like, "I'm sorry you are struggling with that," or "I'm sure that was disappointing to you." Being heard is one of the best gifts you can give to your child.

Perception

Perception is needed throughout the parenting process, but it is especially important during the teen years when kids can easily turn their emotions inward. As hormones invade their bodies and they sort through their place in this world, some kids will be prone to feelings of hopelessness and depression. This is also when eating disorders can begin as well as exposure to drugs and alcohol. It's rare that a child will say, "Mom, Dad, I need help." It's the perceptive parent who watches for signs of unhealthy mental, emotional, and physical patterns and habits. If you perceive something going on inside your teens, don't hesitate to be their advocate and get them the help they need. They may not appreciate it now, but they will thank you later.

Acceptance

Acceptance is of great importance when our children are figuring out their purpose in this world. When we model acceptance, it sets a foundation for their ability to accept themselves, as well. Accept their interests. Accept their strengths. Accept their weaknesses. Accept their failures. Accept the ways they are different from you. Accept their frustrations. As they see you accept yourself and accept them for who they are, they will grow comfortable with the reality of who they are and how God created them.

Love

Love covers it all. The Bible tells us, "Above all, love each other deeply, because love covers over a multitude of sins" (1 Peter 4:8). Loving deeply means resisting the urge to overcorrect. It means choosing grace over criticism. It means allowing them to make mistakes and to suffer natural consequences without adding the consequence of our anger. Loving deeply requires us to have more of God in us than ourselves. Love requires self-control at amazing new levels. Learning to love your imperfect child may be the very thing God uses to bring you to deeper maturity.

WHAT'S MY PURPOSE?

When you tuck your kids into bed, pray for them to know their sense of purpose in this world. Affirm their unique purpose in your family. Give them opportunities to make a difference in the world. While you're at it, tune into your unique purposes as well. The better you know yourself, the better you can know your kids.

CHAPTER 9

WILL YOU *Help* ME CHANGE?

Change isn't easy even for mature adults, so we shouldn't be surprised when our kids struggle to make changes. Kathy and I used our Facebook pages to ask moms why they think change is hard for their kids. Their responses are a great reminder that we're not alone when we're having a hard time getting our kids to grow and mature. Here's a sampling of the responses we got to our "Why is change hard for your kids?" question:

- ✦ Consistency on my part.
- ✦ Getting them to accept "critiques" without seeing them as "criticism."
- ✦ Apathy.

❧ They say "Okay" when you are talking to them but continue doing their own thing.

❧ Fixing it in myself first.

❧ The discipline, patience, and compassion required to experience growth.

❧ Not seeing progress fast enough or struggling when it's two steps forward, one step back.

❧ My lack of perseverance.

❧ I seem to forget my son is only five and expect him to be more capable of understanding certain things.

❧ They don't believe in themselves. They automatically think they can't improve.

❧ Not getting frustrated when you tell them something over and over and it doesn't seem to be getting through!

Raising children well isn't easy. Most kids aren't intentionally bad — not consistently anyway. They're children. They may be childish at times. They will be childlike much of the time. They'll make mistakes because they're learning and growing. They won't do things well when they're initially trying something new.

Remember, the "Come to Momma" mindset we talked about — the one that focuses on progress, not perfection? That mindset is incredibly important for us to remember in managing and motivating change in our children.

ACCEPT, UNDERSTAND, AND ELEVATE THE GOOD

We've talked about acceptance as one of our antidotes to the Perfection Infection. We know it's important in our parenting, but what we also need to realize is that it plays an essential role in our ability to influence our kids. Our kids are likely to resist our input if they believe we don't accept them. Relationship expert John Gottman writes, "Human nature dictates that it is virtually impossible to accept advice from someone unless you feel that that person understands you. . . . It's just a fact that people can change only if they feel that they are basically liked and accepted as they are. When people feel criticized, disliked, and unappreciated they are unable to change."[22]

There's a fine line between rejecting our kids or accepting them while still hoping they'll change, isn't there? Yet that's exactly the tightrope we need to walk as parents. Remember, accepting doesn't always mean agreeing. Accepting simply means acknowledging and recognizing the reality of your child's circumstances. It's being a safe person to be honest with—one who listens, shows compassion and empathy, and leads with love.

How might a child conclude that his parent doesn't accept him? His mom might appear to reject his strengths because she talks about other strengths she wishes he had. If a dad harps on his daughter to change something she's clearly not been able to change, she may feel like she is the problem rather than feeling like a kid with a problem. If a mom becomes negative, pessimistic, and critical because her input doesn't seem to be making a difference, her child may feel rejected and oppose her. Because the child feels rejected, he won't enjoy being in his mom's presence and he won't be open to his mom's input.

Sometimes our kids will experience negative feelings from us when we see some of our negative qualities in them. If we dislike ourselves, we can transfer that to them. Will they sense hopelessness in us? Personal frustration? When we do see ourselves in our kids, is it really okay that we don't have to change but they do? If we think so, we'd better be ready to explain our decision if our older kids confront us. Or will we work for change on the same issue alongside our kids? If we don't, it will naturally be harder for them to change. We'll need to own some responsibility for that.

I've had to undertake that kind of change with my youngest. I'm naturally an introvert who keeps her feelings to herself. In the past I've not been particularly adept at identifying my feelings and tending to them. Sometimes I find myself irritable because of the emotions knotted up inside of me. This has also kept me from being able to be vulnerable in my marriage and with my kids as they've grown older. My youngest is the same way. His emotions get all knotted up inside of him. Both he and I have been using a feelings list (see appendix A) to describe how we're feeling. God is perfecting both of us in the area of communicating our feelings, and it's been more effective to do it together!

When we do see ourselves in our kids, is it really okay that we don't have to change but they do?

Some of what irritates us about ourselves we probably picked up from our parents. It shouldn't surprise us that our children will acquire both positive and negative qualities from us. It's natural and automatic. If we struggle with negativity or anger, it may be a sign we're ready to deal with our own "stuff." If we recognize we're taking anger toward ourselves out on our children, we need to apologize. Then the mature step is to seek help.

What we believe about change is significant, too. We need to see change as possible and even probable. It's helpful to understand that improvement is possible when we know and our kids know both what unhealthy belief or attitude or behavior to remove and what to replace it with. Ephesians 4:22–24 teaches us to take off our old way "which is being corrupted by its deceitful desires" and put on something better "created to be like God in true righteousness and holiness." The 23rd verse includes the very important reality that the mind needs to be renewed for change to stick. Studying relevant concepts in the Bible is best for doing this.[23]

We also need to talk more about the positive behavior we want our child to have than the negative behavior our child is already exhibiting. This helps keep the communication more positive than negative. Joey and Carla Link, authors of *Why Can't I Get My Kids to Behave?*, explained "elevating the good" in a blog post on positive parenting.

> Point your children in the direction you *want* them to go. Instead of saying, "Stop hitting your brother!" try, "Tell me one way you can be nice to your brother." After you get that answer, say, "Are you willing to do that now?" Pointing them to the *good* allows you to get into the habit of saying the opposite of the negative.
>
> Instead of "Stop running in the house!" try "Please walk in the house. You can run outside."
>
> Instead of "Why can't you do what I asked you to do?" try "I asked you to vacuum the family room. When will you get that done?"

....

Instead of "We are late again. Why can't you get your stuff done on time?" try "Make a list of all the things you need to do to get ready to leave the house in the morning."[24]

Joey and Carla encourage parents to write down the negative things you can remember saying to each of your kids this past week. Then reword each statement in a positive way.[25] After all, we are "being perfected," and we have much to learn about elevating the good in our children.

THE ROLE OF COMMUNICATION IN CHANGE

Healthy people and healthy families communicate positively, honestly, completely, and calmly. We demonstrate respect when both speaking and listening. This helps to establish encouragement as the standard in our homes. This type of communication is also essential for passing on truths and values that help our children know why we are asking them to change certain attitudes and behaviors.

If your kids are old enough, share the following concepts with them to stimulate conversation. Which one or two would they like you to work on first? Which one or two would they like to work on first? Teens regularly tell Kathy they often feel like parents have the rule book for the game of life, but expect them to play well without reading it. Discussions about these topics can help them understand the "rule book" for the game of life.

Choose to Be Positive and Optimistic

Beliefs drive behaviors. We can choose to believe someone can change, wants to change, and will change. We can believe we'll be loving,

....

accepting, and successful. Our attitudes are always a choice. Choosing positive beliefs and optimism, even if our last conversation about change was difficult, changes our language, facial expressions, and interactions. We're more welcoming and inviting. We're easier to listen to and change is more likely.

Listen to Learn

Perhaps we have fallen into the pattern of listening just to judge or to hear when someone has finished talking so we can talk. Listen longer, with full attention. Kids resent being interrogated (their word), so we should be careful of peppering them with questions even when we're concerned about their choices and behavior. We may be curious, but we can come across as not trusting and judgmental if we're not careful in how we ask and how we listen. Kids can interpret our many questions as a sign we're anxious. That's one of the things that can increase perfectionist tendencies in kids. Try "Tell me more" or "Keep talking" or "And?" These prompts come across as more respectful and garner more valuable information.

Correct Their Lies

One of the reasons we need to listen to one another carefully is so we can hear and correct their lies. If we overhear our kids lie about themselves to themselves, we must correct them. If we don't and they know we heard them, they'll think we agree with them. They'll accept these labels and identities as truth, decreasing their confidence they can change.

For example, if your son trips and you hear him mumble, "I'm so stupid!" correct him. He's not stupid because he tripped! He may have been clumsy in that moment, or distracted, or in a hurry. Or maybe the corner of the rug was turned up, and anyone would have tripped! You don't want your son to think of himself as stupid. It's just not true. (Follow the same advice if you say a lie to yourself or if you hear one child speak a lie about another.)

Kids can also lie to themselves in the opposite direction. While on the phone with a friend, you may hear your daughter declare, "I know. I can't do anything wrong either." This inflated bragging signals a dangerous belief system because she may no longer be teachable or she may panic when she does make a mistake since she never expects to.

Our power is not in the number of words we use; long lectures are not usually effective.

There are two other kinds of lies to listen for. First, make sure your child doesn't think a temporary situation is permanent. If they do, they won't be motivated to try to improve and they'll definitely resent you asking them to. For instance, just because they have trouble with one math assignment, it doesn't mean they have trouble with math in general. That kind of all-or-nothing thinking is not true. Make sure you model this in your own life. Is your impatience permanent or temporary? How does he hear you talk about it? Is his teasing behavior toward his brother permanent or temporary? When a situation is permanent, talk about the mature choice to change attitudes toward things that can't be changed.

A second type of lie to correct is one regarding causes of strengths and weaknesses. If we hear them proclaim weaknesses are everyone's fault except their own, we'll want to speak into that with the truth. If they blame their siblings every time they get in trouble, they won't be open to our concern about their behavior. It's not true that your children's troubles are everyone else's fault, and it's also not true that their successes belong to others. So don't let your children give away credit for their successes. We don't want our kids to develop pride, but they need to know what they're doing to result in their strengths. Otherwise, they may not believe they can repeat them and they may not recognize a good quality they could use to improve a weakness. For example, a math test wasn't easy because the teacher was in a good mood. It was easy because your daughter listened well in class, asked questions when confused, and took her homework seriously. These are repeatable behaviors that can lead to additional successes when used again.

Talk Briefly

This is a lesson I've learned too often the hard way. Approach communication as a discussion rather than a lecture. As parents, our power is not in the number of words we use. Because of shortened attention spans and the quick pace today's kids are used to, long lectures are not usually effective. It's another Goldilocks moment: not too many, not too few, but just the right amount of words. Here's a tip: if you're starting to get riled up, it's probably time to stop talking and resume the conversation another day. Simply say, "I think we've talked about this enough today. Let's both go and think about it and discuss it some more tomorrow night."

Prioritize Teaching, Not Telling

There's a huge difference between teaching our kids what to do and telling them what to do. Teaching can birth hope. Telling can steal it.

....

Many kids tell Kathy they know what their parents want them to do, but they don't know *how* to do it. This may surprise you. Sometimes our kids may know what to do and choose not to, but many times, they really may not know how to start doing what is necessary. Observe. Look. Listen. Ask. Perceive.

When my kids were old enough to clean a bathroom, I instructed them how to do each part of the cleaning using words and a demonstration, and then I let them do it themselves. I usually gave them at least two times of instruction before I let them do it on their own. This empowered them to do the job right and set the standard for accountability, too.

Teaching will take more words than telling, but we can still be conservative, use our words wisely, and time them well. Essentially, our kids need to know what we want and what we don't want. The contrast of right from wrong can help them figure out when they're wrong and what changes to make. Talking more about what we want than about the current wrong we're observing will help. Answering the "5 Ws and 1 H" makes our explanations complete: What? What is it not? When? Where? Why? And, How?

For example, do they know how to be efficient when setting the table or just that you want them to be? Might your continual complaints about the way they sort their dirty clothes mean they really haven't understood your instructions? Did you tell or teach? Did you do it with them for a while? Were you and they in a positive frame of mind so they could absorb what you were teaching?

Punishment doesn't always change children's behavior. Teaching, modeling, and following through can bring about real change. Yelling certainly doesn't work, but most of us have tried to use it. Michelle Duggar, from the television show *19 Kids and Counting*, shared at a Hearts at Home conference that she learned to stop yelling by replacing yelling with whispering. She said it changed the dynamic in their home. It can be very disarming to make eye contact and say something like, "I love you too much to argue with you. You're too important to me and your heart is too precious. Let's take a break. Let me know when you're ready to be respectful. Then we'll talk more about the attitudes we want you to have toward your sister."

Rewards don't always make changes permanent. They work best when connected to the behavior you're trying to establish. For example, if your kids aren't cooperating, buy a game for the two of them to play together when their behavior improves. If your daughter loves to doodle but was wasting time, give her new colored pencils as a reward for demonstrating better time management skills. Although rewarding kids will sometimes be necessary for them to begin the new behavior, it's healthier to surprise them rather than bribe them. This way, they know their right choices and improvements earned them the surprise. They know they're capable. When we bribe them, they can think they really are incapable and only did better because they wanted the tantalizing bribe we offered. But even when negative and positive consequences work, without instruction on how to behave, chances are the new behaviors won't last.

Correct without Criticizing

When our kids are wrong, we need to correct them and not criticize. Our corrections can be powerfully important to redirect their attitudes, choices, and behaviors. Criticizing won't help. It's demeaning and can suggest they are failures or that we were expecting perfection.

Criticism just points out the wrong. Corrections put it right. Criticisms are negative judgments without any suggestions for how to change. Corrections include instruction. Statements like, "You call that finished?" "I can't believe you just put that there!" and "That attitude is unacceptable" are all criticisms. We've maybe told them what's wrong, but we haven't taught them how to change.

In chapter 6, we shared a three-prong affirmation we can use when complimenting. Being specific, as we explained, helps to create an encouraging culture. With slight adaptations, we can use the same "formula" when correcting, but give it a fourth part. Don't overuse this four-part correction, but use it when you need the extra power to encourage kids to believe they're not failures just because they're doing something wrong.

1. "You are being _____." (Verbalize a specific negative quality you observed. The use of the word "being" helps to suggest the negative quality is temporary and not a part of your child's permanent character.)
2. "I know because _____." (Provide the evidence you saw and/or heard the problem behavior. This makes it easier for them to believe you.)
3. "I'm *not* glad because _____." (The reason you're unhappy your kids behaved in this way can motivate them to change.)
4. "Therefore, _____." (This is where you provide instruction. If you don't include this part of the equation,

you're criticizing and not correcting. You don't say, "Therefore, you will change!" Rather, something like, "You could try this next time: _____." Or ask, "What do you think could help you do something better next time something similar comes up?"

Here's an example: "You are being careless. I know because I found seven simple errors you normally wouldn't make. I'm not glad because we talked before about doing your best. Mistakes because you're confused are one thing. Mistakes because you chose to hurry or not take an assignment seriously are another. Tomorrow, you'll need to begin your homework earlier so we know you have enough time to do your work well. That means fewer minutes gaming, of course."

Here's another example: "You are complaining a lot lately. You let us know you weren't happy to have spaghetti for dinner and then you complained that we wouldn't let you go to Brian's. And you didn't just complain once but several times as if we didn't hear you. We're not glad about your attitude because we're raising you to be grateful. And you know our policy on school nights: You stay home unless there's a school or church function. By asking to go to Brian's, you appeared to ignore us and our family guidelines. We're disappointed in your choices. Please let us know if something else was triggering your complaints because we want to help you. In the meantime, let's each think about gratitude for the next twenty-four hours and come back together tomorrow night to talk again about why we've made that a high value for our family."

Most of us can grow in the area of communication: in our marriages, with our kids, and in other work and personal relationships. This is an area that God does His perfecting work throughout our lifetime. When we learn better interactive skills right along with our kids, it helps them know there's a lifetime of learning ahead for them as well.

CHARACTER COUNTS

In *No More Perfect Moms*, one of the key concepts I shared is the importance of adjusting expectations to better match reality. That concept is important in rooting out Perfection Infection parenting, too. We need to help our kids set appropriate goals. This gives them a target to shoot for and something to aspire to. When we identify something we want them to change, there are two kinds of expectations to stay clear of and one kind of expectation to shoot for. Let's look at all three.

Ability Expectations Don't Work

With ability expectations, children are expected to achieve a certain result because of their natural ability. Ability expectations sound like this: "We expect you to play your recital piece perfectly because you're gifted" and "I know you can earn a perfect score. You're very smart." On the surface, these expectations sound like they'll motivate kids, but they can too easily backfire. Children have no control over their ability. They do have control over how they use their ability — and that's a matter of character. They also have no control over anyone else who can influence the outcome. Ability expectations can actually be quite dangerous. By using them, we teach children to attribute their successes to their ability. But we also teach them to attribute failures to their lack of ability. They can believe they failed because they're stupid. They won't

....

believe they can control that. Therefore, they won't try to change.

Outcome Expectations Don't Work

With outcome expectations, we state an outcome we expect our child to produce. Outcome expectations sound like this: "I know you'll make the debate team" and "You've practiced well. We expect you to win the tournament." But children can't control everything to make our expectations happen. That can be scary and frustrating for them. Kids can do the best they can and still not make the debate team or win the tournament. They can do their best but not meet our expectations. Someone else might debate better at the tryouts. A great player on their team may be ill and that may be the main cause of a team's loss. These expectations suggest we only value results.

Character Goals Do Work

When you set goals that require the use of character, your child is empowered. He learns he can determine his success by choices he makes. Whether he achieves what he set out to or not is dependent upon himself. How others perform doesn't determine whether he is successful. Character goals might include: "Focus on accuracy to increase your math average by five points within the next three weeks" or "We want to see you independently work on your writing longer before you ask for help. Get started with at least three paragraphs of your story before you ask one of us how you're doing or to help you with word choices. We think this will help you gain self-confidence."

Your children will learn to embrace and pursue specific, character-focused goals because they have the internal tools to achieve them.

....

When we state them specifically, there's less confusion. Also these goals allow us to draw attention to the process taking place during the learning and not just the product achieved. It's another reason character goals are more effective than outcome or ability expectations.

When our kids are young, we can communicate what character qualities will help them succeed. When they're older and have had enough experience, they'll figure some out on their own. Our character goal setting will further empower them. They may need to be diligent, patient, focused, positive, careful, optimistic, persistent, and committed to excellence. There are many character qualities you'll want to address and you can find a list of character qualities in appendix D to assist you in character goal setting. If you choose to include character goals as part of your family mission statement, you may want to start talking about them early.

When kids meet their character goals, they'll more likely meet whatever outcome expectations we might have set. This is just a healthier way to get to the successes we want to teach them to value. If they don't meet these goals, they won't be crushed by failure. Rather, they'll know they have the power to make different decisions next time.

We've seen this recently helpful with Kolya, who is now entering the work world. Integrity has been a huge character goal we've been working on with him. Now that he's applying for jobs, interviewing, and having background checks run, he's really starting to understand the value of integrity. There were several lapses of integrity in his life over the past few years that could have netted him a criminal record. However, his mistakes never made it into the court system. The character trait of integrity is now very real to him, and he's realizing that he is the only one who can meet that goal.

In our culture of technology, character goals are especially relevant. They are an effective way to teach some of the character qualities that our kids need in their lives:

- ✦ Diligence: Because technology makes tasks easier (e.g., cut-and-paste, spell-check, search engines) and our kids also multitask using technology, diligence is a quality they may not value as highly as you'd like. Talk with them about not feeling stupid when they are diligent with a long and tedious task. Explain that they work diligently because they care and value themselves. (The same is true for us. Is it possible we haven't persevered with helping our kids improve because we have also bought the technology lie that everything should be easy?)

- ✦ Hard Work: Technology has made mistakes easy to deal with. Kids can quickly undo errors when writing, cancel posts they decide not to share on social media sites even after typing them out, auto-correct pictures, and just turn something off and back on when it stops working. Therefore, they can struggle to invest over time to make improvements. Talk with them about the reality that they can't auto-correct their lives, some learned negative behaviors will take time and effort to change, and some mistakes have consequences that last awhile. We need to make sure we're also modeling these beliefs.

- ✦ Perseverance: Winning is easy on apps and games. We don't ever really lose. We can get a low score or a high score, but we are less likely to think in terms of losing. Winning is a function of time. These days, it's not uncommon to quit halfway through a game because we don't want a low score and we see the writing on the wall. Kids may feel uncomfortable if they think they're not doing well. They may abandon the course rather than have to feel the negative feelings. Calling out perseverance in their lives can help turn that technology lie around.

✦ Self-evaluation: Because of games played and competition television shows watched, our kids expect someone else to tell them how they're doing. As a result, they may not be skilled at self-evaluation. They may be less able to identify when they should change and how to change than we'd like. Increasing their self-smart abilities can help.

STRATEGIES FOR MAKING CHANGE EASIER

Helping our kids change is one of the more important parenting roles we have. Making sure they experience love and security with us even while we're communicating we want better for them is delicate. Loving them for who they are doesn't mean we don't expect more than they're capable of. It does mean, however, we don't expect them to be what they cannot be.

In addition to communicating well and helping our kids set realistic, relevant, and specific goals, there are a few other strategies that can also make it easier for children to change in ways we believe are wise.

Observe for a Solution for Them and You

Ideally, except for issues of safety, don't point out a mistake you see your kids making until you're able to help them change. Otherwise, you'll just be criticizing. Too often we sound like this: "Don't do that." A few minutes pass: "I said, don't do that." Later that day: "I've had it with you! I've told you not to do that!"

Listen and watch longer. Ask yourself: Who's there? What time of day is it? What deadline is this child facing? What kind of a day did he have? What kind of day have I had? Is this something that is changeable or is it something that irritates me, but not my daughter? For her to change, will her brother have to make changes, too? When will I talk with him? What's a possible solution to change her attitude and behavior? How might I change my attitude? Time? Quiet? Attention? Understanding? A character quality? Instruction? A new strategy? When our kids know we'll examine ourselves and not just them *and we'll be looking for solutions and not just problems, they'll be more welcoming and open.*

Expect Your Children to Ask for Specific Help

When kids complain and ask for help with something or say they don't understand, teach them to ask for help specifically. For instance, if your child whines about writing assignments, we might think they need help with the content or organization of their piece. But all they might need is help with spelling. Prevent the drama and teach them how to ask for specific help. Then rarely help them until they do.

Respond Well When They Complain, "I Can't!"

Do you have children who complain, "I can't!" with a long whine they use to their advantage while working on schoolwork, practicing their musical instrument, or doing their daily chores? Maybe they even add, "I'm such a failure/waste/joke." There are two especially helpful responses.

If you notice why they're struggling and their struggle is something you need to own, it's respectful to just take care of it without making a big deal out of it. This is especially true for younger kids or nonverbal kids. It might sound like this: "Oh, you're right. I haven't given you the new cleaning supplies I bought. Sorry about that. Here you go" or, "I can see the problem. Let me remind you where there's more paper."

The other strategy to implement when they say "I can't" is to calmly respond with the question, "What can you do?" Keep a respectful tone of voice and be calm in your response. You'll likely catch them off guard. You're communicating respectfully because you responded to what you heard. When they don't respond, just ask again, "What can you do?" Then listen. Perhaps your daughter will answer, "I can't find the sponge." You can now respond, "That's what you can't do. I asked you, what can you do?" She may respond, "Okay. I get it. I haven't looked in all the places it might be." Perhaps your son will proclaim, "Practicing this song is so boring." You can now respond, "I asked, what can you do?" He will hopefully conclude, "Okay, okay. How about five more minutes?" Your response can be, "No, your teacher expects you to practice thirty minutes, and so do your dad and I, so you have fifteen minutes left. If you hadn't stopped to complain, you'd almost be finished. Do you need me to come help you get restarted?"

Ask Kids What They Want to Improve

Sometimes kids tell Kathy they feel like they're doing nothing right. When they hear their parents ask for improvements or demand change (that's what they hear, whether or not the parent really is demanding), the kids don't know where to start. This is another reason our language needs to be specific.

When the time is right, sit down and have a conversation. Tell your children what is concerning you. Provide evidence and the reason the issue is a problem. One reason might be enough to motivate them. Five reasons might be overwhelming and increase hopelessness. Ask children what they're willing to work on. "Nothing" is not an acceptable answer, but be open to them suggesting something else you didn't verbalize. Choice is a privilege, so if children complain, just decide for them and be directive. If they choose, motivation and focus will increase.

Now watch for improvements in that one area and temporarily back off the others you talked about. Often, just talking calmly will increase the likelihood your kids will work on the other issues, too, so affirm them if you notice that. If they don't seem motivated because it's not a big deal to them, talk about and demonstrate the difference between good, better, and best. Assure them you're not expecting perfection, but you are sure improvements can be made. When progress occurs, ask them how they feel. Getting kids in touch with the emotional satisfaction of improvement and doing well can help them approach other challenges well.

Teach Children Which Strengths and Smarts Are Relevant to Overcoming Problems

Kids need to become aware of their strengths and of how they are uniquely smart. They also need to know which strengths they can apply to the problem they're having. They don't always know. This is, again, where our observing can help.

For instance, children who read dramatically can read out loud to help them remember details from their history assignments. Maybe you're concerned about your daughter's increasing self-centeredness. Talk with her about teaching her logic-smart memorization strategies to others. She may discover that helping others brings a good feeling. Reminding your son he's coordinated and body-smart on the soccer field and picture-smart and body-smart when building with clay can increase his confidence when it's his turn to set the table and fill glasses with tea and milk. Help them see how the gifts they are discovering in themselves can apply in other situations and for other tasks.

Allow Kids to Struggle and Be Disappointed

Throughout these pages, you've found many suggestions designed to help you accept and love your children for who they are. We also suggested many beliefs, attitudes, and actions you need to have and use in order to help your children succeed when they work to overcome challenges. We want you empowered to help them become all God intended for them to be when He chose in His love to make them the way He did.

In the midst of all that encouragement, you'll also have to allow your children to struggle so they can learn to handle disappointment well in the safety and security of your home. Yes, you read that right. If we protect our kids from all pain, they won't learn how to handle it. They'll choose to avoid all struggles and challenges. They'll hit a plateau and stop growing. Then, when they do experience mistakes, failing, and emotional pain, they may crumble. They'll also be more dependent on us during adulthood. (That fact alone should motivate us to let them struggle on occasion!)

Our kids need to experience natural consequences that occur because of what they're doing wrong. This can motivate them to want to change. What you think is a problem they also need to see as a problem. That realization can only happen if we don't rescue them from all negative effects. They need to feel some pain.

For example, if we finish their homework for them because they wasted time earlier in the evening, they're not motivated to learn better time management. If we're helicopter parents, kids don't have to worry about their decisions. They hardly have to think. They know we'll protect them and fix any problems for them. We'll be implying they don't have to be perfect, but our actions will make them perfect. If we're honest, many of the abilities and relationships we value mean a lot to us because we overcame much to arrive at success. We don't want to rob our kids of those same experiences.

PRAY—A LOT!

We know talking to God matters. God gives strength to the weak and wisdom to those who ask (Isaiah 40:29; 2 Corinthians 12:9; James 1:5). He empowers us to love our kids even when we hardly like them. Change is easier when you pray for yourself and pray for your kids.

Prayer is simply talking to God. There's no formula for prayer. No special words are needed. Just talk honestly with God. Tell Him your concerns. Tell Him what you're grateful for. Ask Him for wisdom and direction, and don't be afraid to be specific. What kind of help do you need? What kind of growth do you desire for your kids? God hears all prayers and answers all prayers in the ways that are best. If you'd like some practical help on how to pray specifically for your child, check out appendix C, which shows how you can use God's Word to pray for a child, and appendix D, which provides a list of character qualities you might choose to pray for that child. These will give you a great place to start praying for your child.

Of course, the most powerful prayer is the one we probably least want to pray, "God, change me." Sometimes when there is conflict between me and my child, it's not my child who needs to change. It's me who needs to change. My attitude. My patience. My perspective. My words. My tone of voice. My critical spirit. My anger. Having the courage to pray that prayer and let God do His perfecting work in you is certain to change the relational dynamics between you and your child.

There will be moments in parenting when your disappointment is real. Talk to God about that. He understands because many times His children disappoint Him, too. Your fears for your children may be real. God cares about that too.

You may need to pray each day, "God, help me accept my kids for who they are." Or, as Kathy often jokes with her audiences, maybe your prayer will sometimes be, "God, make me willing to be willing to be willing to be willing to accept my kids for who they are."

THE PROCESS OF BEING PERFECTED

We've covered a lot of ground in the pages of this book. I hope you're able to say in some way that you are not the same as when you started reading. Our prayer is that your compassion has increased, your perception is sharpened, your ability to accept has grown, and your capacity to love unconditionally has expanded.

Change is really about exchange. We replace one thing with something else. What if you and I replaced "being perfect" with "being perfected"? What if we were truly able to embrace that the imperfect parts of our lives are counterbalanced with the reality of a perfect God who longs to shine His light through the cracks in our lives? What if we could believe that fully for ourselves and fully for our children, who are also "being perfected?"

When you and I can let go of "being perfect" and really embrace the process of "being perfected" by God, we'll experience the contentment and freedom we intrinsically long for. We will be content to be ourselves and we'll be content to allow our sons and daughters to be themselves. We'll wish for nothing more than what we already have. Most importantly, we'll find freedom of authenticity for ourselves and we'll give our children the freedom to be themselves.

When I began to embrace God's perfecting work in my own life, I stopped worrying about what people thought. When I stopped worrying about what people thought, I stopped being a controlling parent. When I stopped being a controlling parent, I increased my ability to influence each of my kids by using the Perfection Infection antidotes of compassion, perception, acceptance, and love. Leaving Perfection Infection parenting behind resulted in freedom and contentment in my relationships with my beautifully created, perfectly imperfect children.

Kathy and I hope this book has empowered you to leave Perfection

. . . .

Infection parenting behind. Of course, you won't do it perfectly. You'll revert to old habits on occasion. When you do, admit your mistake and move forward in grace. Thank God for the journey of "being perfected."

As you learn to love your children for who they are, the core questions they internally ask will now have clear answers:

Yes, I like you just as you are.

Yes, you are very important to me.

It's absolutely okay that you are unique.

You are God's beautiful creation.

You're not a failure in any way.

You have incredible value and purpose.

Yes, I'm being perfected, and you are too. I'm glad we get to experience that together.

Feeling WORDS[26]

*T*his list on the following pages may help your children accurately identify feelings they're having that underlie certain behaviors. Using it can expand your children's emotional vocabulary. This can be especially valuable for boys who have many emotional responses to life, but less emotional vocabulary to explain their feelings. For example, when children tell you they're "happy," you could show them all or some of the "happy" words and ask them to choose one or two that most accurately describe their feelings for them at that moment.

HAPPY
Festive
Joyous
Inspired
Glad
Cheerful
Lighthearted
Vivacious
Merry
Jolly
Playful

CONTENT
Satisfied
Comfortable
Peaceful
Tranquil
Pleased
Blessed
Reassured

EXCITED
High-spirited
Elated
Jubilant
Ecstatic
Enthusiastic

Exhilarated

SAD
Sorrowful
Downcast
Dejected
Unhappy
Depressed
Gloomy
Cheerless
Somber
Heavy-hearted
Joyless
Sullen
Moping
Moody
Out of sorts
Ill at ease
Discouraged

CONFUSED
Insecure
Distressed
Nervous
Hesitant
Doubtful
Mixed up

Embarrassed
Puzzled
Perplexed
Misunderstood

HURT
Offended
Grieved
In pain
Injured
Heartbroken
Suffering
Afflicted
Worried
Aching
Crushed
In despair
Devastated
Alone

ANGRY
Resentful
Irritated
Enraged
Furious
Annoyed
Provoked

....

Incensed

Infuriated

Offended

Betrayed

Deceived

AFRAID

Petrified

Fearful

Frightened

Shaky

Apprehensive

Terrified

Panicked

Alarmed

Shocked

Horrified

Worried

Suspicious

Dismayed

Scared

Trembling

Threatened

Doubtful

BRAVE

Encouraged

Courageous

Secure

Daring

Heroic

Self-reliant

Enterprising

Determined

Certain

Bold

Enthusiastic

Confident

Fearless

DOUBTFUL

Unbelieving

Skeptical

Distrustful

Suspicious

Dubious

Uncertain

Questioning

Wavering

Indecisive

Unsure

ANXIOUS

Uneasy

Embarrassed

Frustrated

Ashamed

Nervous

Restless

Worried

Stressed

SURPRISED

Astonished

Amazed

Stunned

Surprised

Shocked

Enlightened

Unaware

Wondering

AGE-APPROPRIATE
Tasks FOR CHILDREN[27]
by Sheila Seifert

What chores are important for your children to learn and what are they capable of doing?

First, recognize the difference between a chore (an ongoing task that benefits the household) and a life skill (an activity that children should know how to do before living on their own, such as managing a checking account). The following list does not include life skills. It is a list of chores.

Second, remember that every child matures at a different pace. Adjust this chart to what you know about your children's skills and talents, and realize that no child should do all of the chores listed below every day.

With those two qualifiers in mind, here are some general guidelines for personal and family chores. This list is only meant as a guide and reflects the types of chores that many children in these age ranges are capable of completing:

AGES 2 AND 3

Personal chores

- ❧ Assist in making their beds
- ❧ Pick up playthings with your supervision

Family chores

- ❧ Take their dirty laundry to the laundry basket
- ❧ Fill a pet's water and food bowls (with supervision)
- ❧ Help a parent clean up spills and dirt
- ❧ Dust

AGES 4 AND 5

Note: Children this age can be trained to use a family chore chart.

Personal chores

- ❧ Get dressed with minimal parental help
- ❧ Make their bed with minimal parental help
- ❧ Bring their things from the car to the house

Family chores

- Set the table with supervision
- Clear the table with supervision
- Help a parent prepare food
- Help a parent carry in the lighter groceries
- Match socks in the laundry
- Answer the phone with parental assistance
- Be responsible for a pet's food and water bowl
- Hang up towels in the bathroom
- Clean floors with a dry mop

AGES 6 AND 7

Note: This age can be supervised to use a family chore chart.

Personal chores

- Make their bed every day
- Brush teeth
- Comb hair
- Choose the day's outfit and get dressed
- Write thank-you notes with supervision

Family chores

- Be responsible for a pet's food, water, and exercise
- Vacuum individual rooms
- Wet mop individual rooms
- Fold laundry with supervision
- Put their laundry in their drawers and closets
- Put away dishes from the dishwasher

❧ Help prepare food with supervision

❧ Empty indoor trash cans

❧ Answer the phone with supervision

AGES 8 TO 11

Note: This age benefits from using a family chore chart.

Personal chores

❧ Take care of personal hygiene

❧ Keep bedroom clean

❧ Be responsible for homework

❧ Be responsible for belongings

❧ Write thank-you notes for gifts

❧ Wake up using an alarm clock

Family chores

❧ Wash dishes

❧ Wash the family car with supervision

❧ Prepare a few easy meals on their own

❧ Clean the bathroom with supervision

❧ Rake leaves

❧ Learn to use the washer and dryer

❧ Put all laundry away with supervision

❧ Take the trash can to the curb for pickup

❧ Test smoke alarms once a month with supervision

❧ Screen phone calls using caller ID and answer when appropriate

AGES 12 AND 13

Personal chores

- ❧ Take care of personal hygiene, belongings, and homework
- ❧ Write invitations and thank-you notes
- ❧ Set their alarm clock
- ❧ Maintain personal items, such as recharging batteries
- ❧ Change bedsheets
- ❧ Keep their rooms tidy and do a biannual deep cleaning

Family chores

- ❧ Change lightbulbs
- ❧ Change the vacuum bag
- ❧ Dust, vacuum, clean bathrooms, and do dishes
- ❧ Clean mirrors
- ❧ Mow the lawn with supervision
- ❧ Babysit (in most states)
- ❧ Prepare an occasional family meal

AGES 14 AND 15

Personal chores

- ❧ Be responsible for all personal chores for ages 12 and 13
- ❧ Be responsible for library card and books

Family chores

- ❧ Do assigned housework without prompting
- ❧ Do yard work as needed

❖ Babysit

❖ Prepare food, from making a grocery list and buying the items (with supervision) to serving a meal occasionally

❖ Wash windows with supervision

AGES 16 TO 18

Personal chores

❖ Be responsible for all personal chores for ages 14 and 15

❖ Be responsible to earn spending money

❖ Be responsible for purchasing their own clothes

❖ Be responsible for maintaining any car they drive (e.g., gas, oil changes, tire pressure, etc.)

Family chores

❖ Do housework as needed

❖ Do yard work as needed

❖ Prepare family meals, from creating the grocery list to serving it, as needed

❖ Deep cleaning of household appliances, such as defrosting the freezer, as needed

HOW TO *Pray* FOR YOUR CHILD USING BIBLE VERSES[28]

Heaven and earth will pass away, but my words will never pass away.

Mark 13:31

PRAY THAT YOUR CHILD . . .

Will be saved

And give _____ one heart [a new heart] and put a new spirit within him/her; and take the stony [unnaturally hardened] heart out of his/her flesh, and give him/her a heart of flesh [sensitive and responsive to the touch of his/her God].

(Adapted from Ezekiel 11:19 AMP)

. . . .

Will return to the Lord

May the Lord give _____ a new heart and put a new spirit in
_____ ; may He remove _____ 's heart of stone and give
_____ a heart of flesh.
(Adapted from Ezekiel 36:26)

Will have courage in difficult tasks

That _____ will be strong and courageous, and do the work. That
he/she won't be afraid or discouraged, for the Lord God, his/her God,
is with _____. Lord, You will not fail _____ or forsake him/her.
You will see to it that all the work . . . of the Lord is finished correctly.
(Adapted from 1 Chronicles 28:20 NLT)

Will walk in faithfulness and devotion

Remember, Lord, how _____ has walked before You faithfully
and with wholehearted devotion and has done what is good in Your
eyes.
(Adapted from Isaiah 38:3)

Will not give up

Let _____ not become weary in doing good, for at the proper time
he/she will reap a harvest if he/she does not give up.
(Adapted from Galatians 6:9)

Will have a gentle spirit

Therefore, as God's chosen people, holy and dearly loved, may _____ clothe himself/herself with compassion, kindness, humility, gentleness, and patience.

(Adapted from Colossians 3:12)

Will stand firm

That _____ may stand firm in all the will of God, mature and fully assured.

(Adapted from Colossians 4:12)

Will be a peacemaker

May _____ be a peacemaker who plants seeds of peace and reaps a harvest of righteousness.

(Adapted from James 3:18 NLT)

Will submit to God and resist the devil

May _____ submit himself/herself, then, to God. Resist the devil, and he will flee from _____ .

(Adapted from James 4:7)

Will not be fearful

So _____ , be strong and courageous! Do not be afraid and do not panic before them. For the Lord your God will personally go ahead of _____. He will neither fail him/her nor abandon him/her.

(Adapted from Deuteronomy 31:6 NLT)

CHARACTER *Qualities* TO DEVELOP IN YOUR CHILDREN[29]

ACCOUNTABILITY: Being answerable to God and at least one other person for my behavior.

ALERTNESS: Being keenly aware of the events taking place around me so that I can have the right responses to them.

AMENDS (Repentance): Humbly acknowledging how you have fallen short of God's standard and seeking His forgiveness to make things right.

ATTENTIVENESS: Showing the worth of a person or task by giving my undivided concentration and effort.

AUTHENTICITY: Being exactly who you claim to be with honesty and transparency.

....

AVAILABILITY: Making my own schedule and priorities secondary to the wishes of those I serve.

BENEVOLENCE: Giving to others' basic needs without expectations of personal reward.

BOLDNESS: Demonstrating the confidence and courage that doing what is right will bring ultimate victory regardless of present opposition.

BONDING: Connecting with one another in an authentic way, avoiding unhealthy isolation.

BOUNDARIES: Creating a "safe place" or limitations that protect me from potentially unmanageable temptation.

BREADTH: Having depth and broadness, in words and deeds, within the heart and mind.

BROTHERLINESS: Exhibiting a kinship and disposition to render help because of a relationship.

CANDOR: Speaking the truth at the time when the truth should be spoken.

CAUTION: Knowing to be alert in a hazardous or dangerous situation.

CHEERFUL: Expressing encouragement, approval, or congratulations at the proper time.

CHIVALRY: Protecting the weak, the suffering, and the neglected by maintaining justice and rightness.

COMMITMENT: Devoting myself to following up on my words (promises, pledges, or vows) with action.

COMPASSION: Investing whatever is necessary to heal the hurts of others by the willingness to bear their pain.

CONFIDENCE: Placing full trust and belief in the reliability of a person or thing.

CONSISTENCY: Following constantly the same principles, course, or form in all circumstances; holding together.

CONTENTMENT: Accepting myself as God created me with my gifts, talents, abilities, and opportunities.

COURAGE: Fulfilling my responsibilities and standing up for convictions in spite of being afraid.

CREATIVITY: Approaching a need, a task, or an idea from a new perspective.

DECISIVENESS: Learning to finalize difficult decisions on the basis of what is right, not on what's popular or tempting.

DEFERENCE: Limiting my freedom to speak and act in order to not offend the tastes of others.

DEPENDABILITY: Fulfilling what I consented to do even if it means unexpected sacrifice.

DETERMINATION: Working intently to accomplish goals regardless of the opposition.

DILIGENCE: Visualizing each task as a special assignment and using all my energies to accomplish it.

DISCERNMENT: Seeking to use intuitive ability to judge situations and people; understanding why things happen to me and to others.

DISCIPLINE: Receiving instruction and correction in a positive way; maintaining and enforcing proper conduct in accordance with the guidelines and rules.

DISCRETION: Recognizing and avoiding words, actions, and attitudes that could result in undesirable consequences.

....

ENDURANCE: Exercising inward strength to withstand stress and to do my best in managing what occurs in my life.

ENTHUSIASM: Expressing lively, absorbing interest in each task as I give it my best effort.

FAIRNESS (EQUITY): Looking at a decision from the viewpoint of each person involved.

FAITH: Developing an unshakable confidence in God and acting upon it.

FAITHFULNESS: Being thorough in the performance of my duties; being true to my words, promises, and vows.

FEAR OF THE LORD: Having a sense of awe and respect for Almighty God that goes above and beyond anyone or anything else.

FIRMNESS: Exerting a tenacity of will with strength and resoluteness. A willingness to run counter to the traditions and fashions of the world.

FLEXIBILITY: Learning how to cheerfully change plans when unexpected conditions require it.

FORGIVENESS: Clearing the record of those who have wronged me and not holding their past offenses against them.

FRIENDSHIP: Coming alongside another person for mutual support and encouragement.

GENEROSITY: Realizing that all I have (time, talents, and treasures) belongs to God and freely giving to benefit others.

GENTLENESS: Learning to respond to needs with kindness, personal care, and love.

GLADNESS: Abounding in joy, jubilation, and cheerfulness.

....

GOAL-ORIENTED: Achieving maximum results toward the area where my effort is directed.

GOODNESS: Having moral excellence and a virtuous lifestyle; a general quality of proper conduct.

GRATEFULNESS: Making known to others by my words and actions how they have benefited my life.

GREATNESS: Demonstrating an extraordinary capacity for achievement.

HOLINESS: Being whole with no blemish or stain.

HONESTY: Proclaiming the truth with sincerity and frankness in all situations.

HONOR: Respecting those in leadership because of the higher authorities they represent.

HOPE: Feeling that my deepest desire will be realized and that events will turn out for the best.

HOSPITALITY: Sharing cheerfully food, shelter, and life with those with whom I come in contact.

HUMILITY: Seeing the contrast between what is perfect and my inability to achieve that perfection.

INDIGNATION: Channeling the driving passion of righteous anger without sinning.

INITIATIVE: Recognizing and doing what needs to be done before I am asked to do it.

INTEGRITY: Being whole and complete in moral and ethical principles.

JOYFULNESS: Choosing to be pleasant regardless of outside circumstances, which ultimately lifts the spirits of others.

. . . .

JUSTICE: Taking personal responsibility to uphold what is pure, right, and true.

KINDNESS: Demonstrating a gentle, sympathetic attitude toward others.

KNOWLEDGE: Becoming acquainted with facts, truths, or principles through study and investigation.

LEADERSHIP: Guiding others toward a positive conclusion.

LOVE: Having a deep personal attachment and affection for another person.

LOYALTY: Using difficult times to demonstrate my commitment to others or to what is right.

MEEKNESS: Yielding my power, personal rights, and expectations humbly with a desire to serve.

NARROWNESS: Staying within established boundaries and limits.

NURTURE: Caring for the physical, mental, and spiritual needs of others.

OBEDIENCE: Fulfilling instructions so that the one I am serving will be fully satisfied and pleased.

OPTIMISM: Confident, hopeful, and never doubtful.

ORDERLINESS: Learning to organize and care for personal possessions to achieve greater efficiency.

ORIGINALITY: Creating "new" thinking and ideas and expanding truths from an independent viewpoint.

PASSIONATE: Having an intense, powerful, or compelling emotion and feelings toward others or something.

PATIENCE: Accepting difficult situations without demanding a deadline to remove it.

PEACEFUL: Being at rest with myself and others.

PERSEVERANCE: A continuing effort to do or achieve something despite difficulties, failure, and opposition.

PERSUASIVENESS: Guiding another's mental roadblocks by using words that cause the listener's spirit to confirm the spoken truth.

POISE: Being totally balanced in mind, body, and spirit.

PRAYERFUL: Communing with God spiritually through adoration, confession, thanksgiving, and supplication.

PROSPERITY: Flourishing or being successful, especially pertaining to financial issues.

PRUDENCE: Exhibiting caution, humbleness, and wisdom in regard to practical matters.

PUNCTUALITY: Showing respect for other people by respectfully using the limited time they have.

PURE SPEECH: Speaking words that are clean, spotless, and without blemish.

PURITY: Freeing yourself from anything that contaminates or adulterates.

PURPOSEFUL: Exercising determination to stay on track until the goal is achieved.

REASONABLENESS: Having a sound mind by being level-headed, sane, and demonstrating common sense.

RENEWAL: Restoration of strength through recovery and replenishment.

RESOURCEFULNESS: Using wisely that which others would normally overlook or discard.

RESPECT: Honoring and esteeming another person due to deep admiration.

RESPONSIBILITY: Knowing and doing what is expected from me.

RESTORATION: Getting a fresh start or new beginning.

REVERENCE: Giving honor where it is due and respecting the possessions and property of others.

RIGHTEOUSNESS: Acting in a moral and upright way that honors God, regardless of who is watching.

SECURITY: Structuring my life around what is eternal and cannot be destroyed or taken away.

SELF-CONTROL: Bringing my thoughts, words, actions, and attitudes into constant obedience in order to benefit others.

SENSITIVITY: Being aware and attentive to the true attitudes and emotional needs of those around me.

SERVANTHOOD: Caring for and meeting the needs of others before caring for self.

SINCERITY: Endeavoring to do what is right without ulterior motives.

STEWARDSHIP: Administering and managing personal and financial affairs effectively.

STRENGTH: Having power, force, and vigor for the task assigned.

SURRENDER: Yielding to the authority, guidance, and direction of God in my life.

TEACHABILITY: Demonstrating a willingness to learn or be trained without any reservations or hindrances.

THANKFULNESS: Expressing deep gratitude and appreciation to people and to God.

THOROUGHNESS: Executing something perfectly with the realization that each of my tasks will be reviewed.

THOUGHTFULNESS: Showing consideration for others through acts of kindness and/or words.

THRIFTINESS: Preventing myself or others from spending money unnecessarily.

TOLERANCE: Learning to accept others as valuable individuals regardless of their maturity.

TRANSPARENCY: Allowing others to shine a light on my life for the purpose of being accountable.

TRUST or TRUSTWORTHY: Believing completely and totally in someone or something.

TRUTHFULNESS: Earning future trust by accurately reporting past facts.

UNDERSTANDING: Exhibiting strong intelligence and a sound mind in comprehending and discerning matters.

UNSTOPPABLE: The freedom to perform at your highest level without any restraints.

VIRTUE: Building personal moral standards that will cause others to desire a greater moral life.

VISIONARY: Dreaming not inhibited by the unknown. Looking beyond problems by creating successful solutions.

VULNERABILITY: Being open to receiving constructive criticism and guidance.

WISDOM: Learning to see and respond correctly to life situations with keen judgment; the application of knowledge.

WORSHIP: Honoring God reverently.

SCRIPTURAL *Blessings* TO PRAY[29] FOR YOUR CHILDREN

by Brian Smith

*B*lessing our children is part of a rich biblical heritage. In the Old Testament, fathers regularly pronounced blessings on their children (see Genesis 27:26–29, 39–40, 49:1–28). As New Testament believers and priests of God (1 Peter 2:9), one of our privileges is to bless others. When we invoke God's name over His people, God blesses them (see Numbers 6:22–27).

As you pray these blessings for your children, consider pronouncing them aloud, as Old Testament parents did. Hearing you claim God's blessings on their lives will build your children's faith, remind them of their true God-given identity, and reinforce your—and their heavenly Father's—great love for them.

....

Assurance of salvation. Lord, lead my children to trust only in Jesus' sacrifice for their eternal salvation; assure them that their souls are secure in Your hands. (John 3:16, 10:28–29; 1 John 5:13)

Intimacy with God. Draw my children face-to-face with You, that they might taste Your goodness and long for more of You. (Exodus 33:11; Psalm 27:8, 34:8, 42:1–2)

Spiritual blessings. Father, remind my children that You have adopted them in love. Enable them to experience all the spiritual blessings they have in Christ Jesus, especially Your measureless love. May they act, speak, and think in ways fitting for a child of God. (Ephesians 1:3–14, 3:17–19, 5:8–10)

Confidence in prayer. Assure my children that You hear their prayers and that You always answer as a caring Father, even when they do not receive what they want. (1 John 5:14–15; Matthew 7:7–11)

Repentance. When my children sin, quickly lead them to confess and repent so that they might enjoy a clear conscience and unbroken fellowship with You. (Psalm 32:1–2; 1 John 1:5–9)

Sanctification. Transform my children into Christ's likeness. Use whatever circumstances You, in Your perfect wisdom, deem necessary to produce a harvest of righteousness and peace in their lives. (2 Corinthians 3:18; James 1:2–4; Hebrews 12:5–11)

Hope and rest. Bathe my children in restful, confident hope as they trust You with their self-worth, relationships, life's work, and _____ (other concerns). May they overflow with Your peace. (Jeremiah 29:11; Matthew 28–30; Romans 15:13, Philippians 4:6–7)

Comfort. Through every hardship, may Your Spirit bring tangible consolation to my children so that they will know that they are not alone. Right now, they need Your comfort to get through _____ (pray for specific trials or losses). (Matthew 5:4; John 14:16–18)

....

Freedom. Guide my children into truth so that they will enjoy genuine freedom. (John 8:31–32, 36)

Friendships. Provide my children with friends who are supportive and truthful. Keep them from relationships that would draw them away from You. (Ecclesiastes 4:9–12; Proverbs 27:5–6; 1 Corinthians 15:33)

Effective parents. Help me (and my spouse) to be the influence my children need at every stage of their growth. Keep me willing to listen to anything they want to discuss. (Proverbs 20:7; Ephesians 6:4)

Marriage and children. If it is Your will that my children marry and have children, guide them to godly spouses with whom they will enjoy flourishing relationships. May they pass along a rich heritage to future generations. May those who remain single experience the joy of living in undivided devotion to You. (Psalm 127:3–5, 128:1–4; 1 Corinthians 7:32–35)

A healthy church. Provide my children with a unified, prayerful, Bible-teaching church family that will draw them into community, give them a hunger for Your Word, and involve them in Your work; bless them with spiritual leaders who are trustworthy and humble. (Acts 2:42, 4:32–35; Ephesians 4:15–16; 1 Timothy 3:1–13)

Holy Spirit. Fill my children with Your Holy Spirit. Show them how to exercise their spiritual gifts, and enable them to bear all the fruit of Your Spirit—love, joy, peace, patience, kindness, goodness, faithfulness, gentleness, and self-control. (Ephesians 5:18; 1 Corinthians 12:4–28; Galatians 5:22–23)

Influence. Lord, may my children attract many to You as they influence the world with truth and righteousness. (Matthew 5:13–16; Mark 1:17; 2 Corinthians 2:15–16)

Success. As they study and apply Your Word, may my children bear much eternal fruit. Grant them success in _____ (specific God-honoring endeavors). (Joshua 1:7–8, John 15:8; James 1:25)

Wisdom. Bless my children with wisdom, and give them a constant hunger for more. Fill them with the knowledge of Your Word and Your will. Grant them a life-giving fear of You, for that is where all wisdom begins. (Proverbs 3:13; James 1:5; Colossians 1:9; Proverbs 9:10)

Guidance. By the Holy Spirit's power, lead my children along paths of righteousness. Specifically, guide them in _____ (circumstances your children currently face). (Proverbs 3:5–6; John 16:13)

Protection. Keep my children physically safe and healthy, and guard them from the evil one. Help them resist _____ (specific current or future temptations). (James 5:14–16; John 17:15; 2 Thessalonians 3:3; 1 Corinthians 10:13)

Provision. Supply my children's earthly needs. At the moment they need _____. (Matthew 6:11, 25–33; Philippians 4:19)

Eternity. Remind my children of the eternal rewards You promise. Let this perspective motivate them to lay up treasure in heaven. May they seek first Your kingdom and righteousness by living with integrity and investing generously in the lives of people. (1 Corinthians 3:12–14; 2 Corinthians 5:1, 10; John 14:2–3; Matthew 6:19–21, 33)

The unimaginable. Gracious Father, shower my children with blessings that exceed my dreams. May Your love flow abundantly into their lives. (Ephesians 3:17–20)

RECOMMENDED READING
FOR *Perfectly*
IMPERFECT KIDS

*C*hildren's books are fun to read to children and beneficial for them to read to themselves. Not only can teaching and learning take place because of rich content, but children report rarely feeling more secure than they do while cuddling with parents and a good book.

Check the books you already own and favorites you check out from the library for themes we've addressed in this book. Use the characters and situations they find themselves in to begin discussions and then, as appropriate, bring the discussion around to include you and your children. Take advantage of these teachable moments.

· · · · · · · ·

In addition to the books listed here to get you started, one of our favorite resources for books is *The Read-Aloud Handbook* by Jim Trelease (Penguin Books). Also ask your children's librarian and children's teachers for recommendations.

The Boy Who Changed the World by Andy Andrews (Nelson), ages 4–8 (purpose)

Old Hat, New Hat by Stan and Jan Berenstain (Random House), ages 2–6 (identity)

The Big Red Tractor and the Little Village by Francis Chan (David C. Cook), ages 4–8 (purpose, strengths)

Ronnie Wilson's Gift by Francis Chan (David C. Cook), ages 4–8 (purpose)

You Are My I Love You by MaryAnn Cusimano (Penguin Putnam), ages 3–5 (love)

The Day the Crayons Quit by Drew Daywalt (Philomel), ages 3–7 (purpose, uniqueness, strengths and weaknesses, importance)

The Crayon Box That Talked by Shane Derolf (Random House), ages 3–7 (purpose, identity)

The Matchbox Diary by Paul Fleschman (Candlewick), ages 6–10 (purpose, uniqueness, importance, change)

My Name Is Not Isabella: Just How Big Can a Little Girl Dream? by Jennifer Fosberry and Mike Litwin (Sourcebook Jabberwocky), ages 4–8 (purpose, identity)

Even If I Did Something Awful by Barbara Shook Hazen (Macmillan/Aladdin), ages 3–6 (failure, love)

Chester's Way by Kevin Henkes (Greenwillow Books), ages 4–8 (identity, uniqueness)

....

Chrysanthemum by Kevin Henkes (Mulberry Books), ages 3–5 (uniqueness, labels, bullying)

The Tale of Three Trees by Angela Elwell Hunt (David C. Cook), ages 4–11 (purpose, uniqueness)

Accidents May Happen: Fifty Inventions Discovered by Mistake by Charlotte Jones (Delacorte), ages 8–12 (purpose, strengths, failure)

A Porcupine Named Fluffy by Helen Lester (Houghton Mifflin Harcourt), ages 4–8 (identity, uniqueness)

Tacky the Penguin by Helen Lester (Houghton Mifflin Harcourt), ages 4–8 (uniqueness)

Pete the Cat: I Love My White Shoes by Eric Litwin (HarperCollins), ages 3–6 (change)

Gus, the Dinosaur Bus by Julia Liu (Houghton Mifflin Harcourt), ages 3–8 (importance, purpose, strengths and weaknesses)

A Hat for Ivan by Max Lucado (Crossway), ages 4–8 (importance, uniqueness, love)

Best of All by Max Lucado (Crossway), ages 4–8 (importance, purpose, strengths, love)

If I Only Had a Green Nose by Max Lucado (Crossway), ages 4–8 (uniqueness, purpose, bullying)

Just the Way You Are by Max Lucado (Crossway), ages 4–8 (acceptance, love)

The Oak Inside the Acorn by Max Lucado (Crossway), ages 5–10 (importance, purpose, uniqueness)

The Tallest of Smalls by Max Lucado (Nelson), ages 4–7 (uniqueness, acceptance)

. . . .

You Are Mine by Max Lucado (Crossway), ages 4–8 (importance, purpose, uniqueness, love)

Sophie's Squash by Pat Zietlow Miller (Schwartz & Wade), ages 3–7 (change, importance, purpose)

The Kissing Hand by Audrey Penn (Tanglewood), ages 3–8 (reassurance, love)

The Little Engine That Could by Watty Piper (Grosset & Dunlap), ages 3–5 (identity, purpose, failure)

You're Wearing That to School? by Lynn Plourde (Disney-Hyperion), ages 4–8 (uniqueness, labels, friendship)

Thank You, Mr. Falkner by Patricia Polacco (Philomel), ages 5–8 (strengths and weaknesses, special needs)

I Believe in You by Marianne Richmond (Sourcebooks) ages 4–8 (importance, uniqueness, purpose, power of belief)

It's Not Easy Being a Bunny by Marilyn Sandler (Beginner Books/ Random House), ages 3–7 (uniqueness, identity)

Don't Laugh at Me by Steve Seskin and Arthur Shamblin (Tricycle Press), ages 3–7 (uniqueness, special needs, bullying)

The Library by Sarah Stewart (Square Fish), ages 5–9 (strengths, interests, purpose)

Inside Outside Who We Are by Steve Tiller, ages 3–9 (uniqueness, identity, importance, special needs)

Just Be Yourself! by Steve Tiller (Michaelsmind), ages 3–9 (uniqueness, identity, importance, strenths, purpose, special needs)

The Snoodle's Tale by Phil Vischer (Zonderkidz), ages 4–7 (uniqueness, purpose, strengths)

A Funny Little Bird by Jennifer Yerkes (Sourcebooks), ages 4–8 (identity, change, uniqueness, purpose, strengths and weaknesses)

....

LEADER'S GUIDE

*D*ear Leader,

Hearts at Home (www.HeartsatHome.org) is an organization built on the premise that parents are most effective when they're not going it alone. So one of the primary goals of your group should be building supportive relationships. We pray your parents group will find *No More Perfect Kids* a great text for launching life-changing discussions.

The group sessions are organized around the nine chapters, so you should try to plan for nine group meetings. Encourage each family to have a copy of the book so that moms and dads can highlight or mark their copies as they read—and bring their marked-up copies to your group meetings.

The leader's job is to facilitate discussion, and the best group leaders prefer hearing others talk more than listening to themselves. You can't be a perfect leader, but we hope you'll try to be as authentic as possible. Although you may lead by example in answering the questions yourself, you should try to drive the discussion and life-application deeper.

In your preparation time, familiarize yourself with the questions and jot down any additional questions you might present to the group. Pray for group members and for God's guidance.

In your Dig Deep time, do your best to draw out the quieter group members and to move the discussion along if one parent tends to monopolize the conversation. If the group gets off the subject, pull the focus back to the question posed.

The Apply section encourages personal reflection and goal-setting. It would be great for group members to go home with one piece of wisdom they want to assimilate into their parenting that week—and some ideas for actions they might take to make the teaching real in their families.

Be sure to make time for prayer, either having one person close in prayer or sharing a group prayer time. If your group is not really comfortable with praying together, you as the leader may have to take that responsibility of closing in prayer.

We pray God blesses your group as you embrace your own imperfections and cultivate love and acceptance in your various families.

Introduction/Chapter 1: No More Perfect Kids

Dig Deep

1. Jill offers snapshots of times when her parenting expectations clashed with the reality she faced (pp. 19–21). Can you identify a moment in your parenting experience when you were up against something you'd never expected?

2. In the situations described, how did you work through your own frustration or disappointment?

3. We've said that "attempts aren't failure; they are part of life." How can it be exasperating to cope with progress instead of perfection? How might it be a relief to embrace progress as an ideal rather than perfection?

4. What happens when goals for your children are set too low? too high? When have you struggled with setting expectations that are "just right"?

5. Does the Greener Grass Syndrome ever rob you of your content-ment? When do you catch yourself comparing yourself, your home, your family with others? When have you been able to be content with life *as it is* and your kids *as they are*? What difference does it make?

....

Apply

6. Recall your own clashes between parenting expectations and reality. How do you feel about the way you handled those instances? If you are still berating yourself for past mistakes, remember that you are imperfect (just like your kids!) and let those old experiences go, asking God to help you in the future.

7. Try to identify a particular area of parenting struggle, maybe over an ongoing issue in which your expectations are not being met. Take another look at your expectation — and your child's unique personality. Could your expectation be too high? If the expectation is reasonable, how might you encourage your child's progress (baby steps!) toward meeting the expectation?

8. Quickly jot down a short list of things you like about your life *as it is* and your kids *as they are*. Use that list this week to pray your thanks to the Lord for the things that are going well for your family.

Pray

Thank God for His patient, understanding love for you, His imperfect child. Thank Him for the real kids that He purposely gave to you, the best parent for the job. Ask God to give you keen insight into your children, so that you discern how to set fair and appropriate goals. Ask God for the wisdom He promises to give (James 1:5).

········

Chapter 2: The Perfection Infection Collides with Parenting

Dig Deep

1. When do you most notice the inundation of perfection around you? In what ways has perfectionism sneaked up to infiltrate your thinking and reactions?

2. Review the ten dangers of perfectionism covered on pp. 38–45. Some patterns in your parenting have grown out of your own experience as you grew up. When you were a child, did you tend to focus on your weaknesses? Did you feel criticized? Were you afraid to ask your parents and teachers for help?

3. When have you personally felt that you were loved unconditionally? How do you think that experience has helped you understand God's love for you?

4. What are the practical differences between excellence and perfection?

Apply

5. Either because life is so hectic or because we are natural "fixers," it's easy to jump straight into solving problems as they arise. This week, when your child tells you about issues that have come up at school or at home, how might you create the time for listening and conveying empathy?

········

6. Four actions can increase your perception of your child's heart attitudes: Think, Engage, Listen, and Wait. When have you seen past your child's outward behaviors to the child's underlying feelings and attitudes? What difference did it make?

7. Create a short list of things you love and appreciate about your child. How might you communicate your joy in his or her uniqueness?

8. Revisit 1 Corinthians 13:4–7. How could this practical description of love help you communicate your unconditional love for your child?

Pray

Thank God for His unconditional love for you, even if it's hard for you to feel that love. Thank Him for loving your children, even more than you do! Ask God to help you enjoy the unique personality and gifts of your children. Ask Him to help you see past the surface behaviors to all-important heart issues. Ask God for his grace to help you pattern your love after 1 Corinthians 13.

Chapter 3: Do You Like Me?

Dig Deep

1. Even if we think we have set aside our earlier dreams of our future children, sometimes those dreams linger to affect our parenting. When have you caught yourself parenting the child you wish you had rather than the one you really were given?

2. When have you felt invisble? misunderstood? disrespected? What feelings accompanied those experiences?

3. When have your children totally surprised you with their hopes and dreams—that is, hopes and dreams very different from the ones you've held for them? How did you respond? Is there anything you want to do differently in the future?

4. In setting goals for your child, how have you balanced appropriate parental guidance and the child's expressed desires? Are there times when your good desires for your kids should become "ruling desires"? When? Why or why not?

Apply

5. How might you "grieve what isn't" in your family—that is, the dreams or expectations you held that have not been realized? What helps you give yourself grace as you let go of those old dreams?

. . . .

6. Do you find it easy or difficult to be transparent with your kids about your own struggles? What would help you feel safe enough to be vulnerable with them?

7. What things about your child would you like to change? Categorize those issues. Are they really critical issues that must be changed for the child's ultimate well-being? Are they issues that bug you but really aren't worth clashing over? Are some of these personality traits or personal choices you can accept?

8. What do you love about your child? Does your child see those rich gifts in himself or herself? How might you help your child identify what's great about him or her? What difference might it make?

Pray

Thank God for the dreams and hopes you have for your child—and thank Him for the ones you've had to let go, too. Thank Him for His grace and compassion toward you. Ask God to help you absorb His grace so that you can communicate similar love and acceptance to your children. Ask God to help you "love without stopping" even when you are frustrated or angry.

Chapter 4: Am I Important to You?

Dig Deep

1. How have your own feelings of importance (or lack of them) affected your behavior and choices?

2. What factors make children (and later, adults) feel unimportant? When have you felt most known and valued by others? How did this affect you?

3. If every person's core needs are security, identity, belonging, purpose, and competence, why is it a problem to look for fulfillment of these needs in parenting?

Apply

4. "Children can feel like projects their parents are trying to finish or problems they're trying to solve—instead of children in the process of becoming." What aspects of parenting are very much like working on projects and solving problems? What can help our children realize that, even in the practical nitty-gritty of preparing them for life, we love them and value their growing-up journeys?

5. What are practical differences between teaching a child to change and telling the child to change?

6. In heavily scheduled family life, it can be a challenge to get past the urgent demands of work, school, and housekeeping to make time just to be together with your child with no other agenda. How might you work in time to play or relax together this week? Why is this worth doing?

7. Without letting your child direct the activities and atmosphere of your family life, how might you enlarge his or her importance in family conversation and decision making?

Pray

Thank God for making you in His own image (Genesis 1:26–27), for creating you (Psalm 139), and for loving you and providing for your salvation (Romans 5:8). Thank Him for giving you security, identity, and belonging in relationship with Him. Ask God to help you see, value, and affirm your child's importance in your family and in the world.

Chapter 5: Is It Okay I'm Unique?

Dig Deep

1. Was there some aspect of your own personality or appearance that you disliked when you were a child? How did you come to accept that trait or realize why God might've made you just the way He did?

2. Check out the chart on p. 120. As you sort out your own characteristics, what kinds of "smart "are you? How have you been able to accept that not EVERY kind of smart is a strength?

3. Reread 1 Corinthians 12:4–27 (printed on pp. 122–23). What has been your experience of "body life" with other Christians? In what ways have you been able to work together and support each other?

Apply

4. Jot your children's names on a sheet of paper, followed by the types of smart you think each might be. How might you reinforce and encourage each child's natural "bent"?

5. As you identify your children's smarts, do you feel any disappointment or frustration because their gifts are so different from your own or because their gifts are not the ones you'd hoped for them? How can you give yourself some grace as you grieve and move on? Why is this worth doing?

6. Since children "catch" so much from watching the example of their parents, how might you bring up your own strengths and weaknesses with your kids this week? What stories from your own struggle might encourage them in their process of becoming?

7. The family is the first place we live out the "one-another" commands of Scripture that build the church as the interconnected, interdependent body. Consider the varied strengths and weaknesses represented in your immediate family. Can you see in that mix of gifts any opportunities for building the support and interdependence of a body?

Pray

Thank God for His wisdom and sovereignty over the unique characteristics of you and of your children. Thank him specifically for the smarts you see represented in your family. Ask God to give you wisdom for helping your children grow in their areas of giftedness. Ask God to help you strengthen each member of your family for healthy "body life" within your immediate family and within the family of God.

Chapter 6: Who Am I?

Dig Deep

1. What labels/nicknames have you carried in the past?: (See the list from pp. 134–35. "Oldest, youngest, middle child. Adopted. ADHD. Anxious. Prodigal. Smart. Thinker. Feeler. Introvert. Extrovert. Talker. Quiet. Verbal. Funny," etc.) Were some of the labels helpful or positive? Which ones have stuck with you the longest? Why?

2. Which of the labels were "doing" labels—that is, based on things you do or achieve? Which of them were "being" labels—based on character, who you are?

3. How do you think your own relationship with your dad influenced your beliefs, choices, and personality?

4. When has another person's affirmation been life-changing for you?

Apply

5. Think about each of your children. Do you think they see themselves as mistakes or as unique, one-of-a-kind, unrepeatable miracles? What affects the way they see themselves?

6. Review the description of the three-prong affirmation (p. 140). Brainstorm, and map out a way you might affirm one positive character

....

trait for each of your kids using the formula (verbalize a specific positive quality, provide evidence to back up your assertion, and give the reason you're so glad about it).

7. Think back to your interaction with your kids in the past week, which probably included some "doing labels" or "being labels." Give yourself some grace if you feel now that there were negative labels in that mix. Think ahead to situations that might come up in the next few days and choose affirming ways to communicate.

Pray

Thank God for His grace and mercy, fresh for you every day (new every morning). Thank God for creating your children and creating you as unrepeatable miracles. Ask God to help you increasingly see and celebrate the goodness of His work in creating each member of your family—and in putting you together.

Chapter 7: Am I a Failure?

Dig Deep

1. When does perfectionism keep you from relaxing in the knowledge that you are being perfected by God, in His timing?

2. Are you especially hard on yourself when you make mistakes? Do you find it hard to forgive yourself, to give yourself some compassion and grace? Are there reasons that would be worth discovering?

3. Review the reasons given on pp. 156–59 about why kids make mistakes. Could some of these be the same reasons *you* make mistakes? What might help you cut yourself some slack and move forward?

4. Would you characterize yourself as more optimistic or pessimistic? How might you practice "spin doctoring" experiences toward taking the most hopeful view and expecting the best outcomes?

5. Who are the people in your life that you respect because they have overcome struggles or difficult situations? How did their challenges help make them who they are?

Apply

6. Do you think your kids feel safe making mistakes at your house? What might help them share more freely when things go wrong for them?

7. Life can get so busy that it's hard to find time to get past the logistics of family schedules to talk with our kids about their feelings. Think about the week ahead. When are some times when you might snatch a chance to talk one-on-one with each of your kids? How do you think they'll respond to this idea?

8. Regularly sharing relaxed moments together builds a nice foundation for the times when you've got to share struggles and disappointments as a family. If it's been awhile since your family scheduled some shared downtime, look for a place to get fun into the calendar in the week ahead.

Pray

Thank God for His gracious forgiveness for you. Thank Him for giving you strength and courage and wisdom in your parenting. Ask Him to give you grace as you handle mistakes in your family (yours and your kids').

Chapter 8: What's My Purpose?

Dig Deep

1. What activities excite and fulfill you most? How are these activities connected with the purposes you feel God has given you?

2. Ephesians 2:10 suggests that God has prepared in advance "good works" for us to do. What are some of the "good works" God has already given you to do, past or present? How do you feel when using them?

3. At what times and during which activities do you sense that you are glorifying God in your actions?

4. What is your favorite way to serve others? Why?

Apply

5. What are some ways you praise God as a family? How can everyday tasks be acts of worship? (Romans 12:1)

6. How do you and your family members cope with boredom? If "screen time" has become a default escape, how could you incorporate more productive and interpersonal pastimes?

7. Begin brainstorming a quick survey of your children. What things

do they do well? What do they get excited about? What dreams do they have?

8. How might your kids' particular interests and gifts lend themselves to some outlet for serving others? Are these projects you might tackle as a family?

Pray

Thank God for His plans for you and for your individual children. Thank Him for creating good works in advance for you to do. Ask God for wisdom in supervising your own time and your children's use of their time. Ask God to bring you opportunities to put to service the range of gifts represented in your family.

Chapter 9: Will You Help Me Change?

Dig Deep

1. Who are the people in your life who have invested in helping you grow to maturity? Who have been good truth-tellers for you, helping correct your misconceptions about yourself or the world around you or shedding the light of God's Word on issues that have come up in your life? How did this matter to you?

2. Are there any lies a child might be believing about him or herself? How might you be able to speak truth into that lie? What might convince your child you are correct?

3. As an adult, how do you feel about change? Do you find it challenging—or even nearly impossible? Do you feel hopeful about it? Why or why not?

Apply

4. Healthy family communication is positive, honest, complete, and calm (p. 198). How would you rate your interactions with your kids in these four areas? Is there one area that you would choose to focus on improving in the week ahead?

5. Some children are harder to draw out in conversation. During what activities and at what times of day do your best conversations with

. . . .

your kids come up? How might you capitalize on that knowledge and help to create time and space for good talks?

6. How do you see the differences between *teaching* and *telling* (p. 201) and between *correcting* and *criticizing* (p. 203)?

7. Can you identify a specific challenge your child faces right now? Which of your child's strengths and smarts might help him or her overcome that problem? How might you help your child identify those gifts and possible solutions?

Pray

Thank God that He has promised His grace to be sufficient in our weaknesses (2 Corinthians 12:8–12). Thank Him for making you more and more like Christ (2 Corinthians 3:17–18; Ephesians 4:23–25). Trust Him with the maturing process of your individual children. Ask God to give you special discernment in coming alongside your children in their work to grow in Christ.

NOTES

Cheri's Story

1. Cheri Nixon, blog post "Perfection Is an Ugly Word," July 17, 2013. Used by permission. www.hecticsweetness.com.

Chapter 2: The Perfection Infection Collides with Parenting

2. Jill Savage, *No More Perfect Moms* (Chicago: Moody Publishers, 2012), 18–19.

3. Ibid.

4. Ibid.

5. Ibid.

6. These teaching points are adapted from a Hearts at Home presentation by Susan Merrill, author of *The Passionate Mom* (Nashville: Thomas Nelson, 2013).

7. Adapted from Dani Dipirro, blog post, "What If You Accepted People Just as They Are," Positively Present, November 2011, www.positivelypresent.com.

8. Savage, *No More Perfect Moms*, 63–65.

········

Leah's Story

9. Leah Courtney, blog post, "Just When You Thought You Had This Parenting Thing Down," July 18, 2013, www.courtneysix.blogspot.com. Used by permission.

Chapter 3: Do You Like Me?

10. Paul Tripp, "How to Be Good and Angry" video series.

Chapter 4: Am I Important to You?

11. Isaiah 64:8; Psalm 139:13.

12. Psalm 139:14; Ephesians 2:10.

13. John 5:24; Romans 5:8; Ephesians 2:8–9.

14. Dr. Kathy's book *Finding Authentic Hope and Wholeness: Five Questions That Will Change Your Life* (Chicago: Moody Publishers, 2005), unpacks these five core needs in great detail.

Connie's Story

15. Connie Johnson, blog post, "My Kid Doesn't Meet My Expectations," July 18, 2013. Used by permission. http://conniedavisjohnson.com.

Chapter 5: Is It Okay if I Am Unique?

16. Kathy Koch, *How Am I Smart? A Parent's Guide to Multiple Intelligences* (Chicago: Moody Publishers, 2007).

Laura's Story

17. Laura Wells, blog post, "When You Care about Your Daughter's Appearance More Than You Want To," July 11, 2013. www.pruningprincesses.com. Used by permission.

Chapter 6: Who Am I?

18. Craig Groeschel, *Altar Ego: Becoming Who God Says You Are* (Grand Rapids: Zondervan, 2013), 23.

Christy's Story

19. Christy Hammer. Used by permission.

Chapter 7: Am I a Failure?

20. Dictionary.Reference.com.

Chapter 8: What's My Purpose?

21. See come&live.com.

Chapter 9: Will You Help Me Change?

22. John Gottman, *The Seven Principles for Making Marriage Work: A Practical Guide from the Country's Foremost Relationship Expert* (New York: Three Rivers Press, 1999).

23. For a detailed description of how to use the Scriptures to renew the mind, see Dr. Kathy's book *Finding Authentic Hope and Wholeness* (Chicago: Moody Publishers, 2005), chapter 5.

24. Joey and Carla Link, guest blog post, "Positive Parenting," June 27, 2013, www.jillsavage.org.

25. Joey and Carla Link, *Why Can't I Get My Kids to Behave?* (Bloomington, IN: WestBow Press, 2013).

Feeling Words

26. Material developed by Dr. Kathy Koch.

Age-Appropriate Tasks for Children

27. Excerpted from the article "Age-Appropriate Chores" by Sheila Seifert. Copyright © 2009, Focus on the Family. Used by permission.

How to Pray for Your Child Using Bible Verses

28. All rights reserved. Moms in Prayer International, 2013. Used by permission.

Character Qualities to Develp in Your Children

29. Adapted from several sources, including *The Institute in Basic Conflicts*, the *Character First!* Program, *The Character of Jesus* by Charles Edward Jefferson (Hong Kong: Forgotten Books, 2012), and the teaching of Bruce Bickel. Reprinted from *Character That Counts: Who's Counting Yours?* (2012) by Rod Handley. Used by permission of Cross Training Publishing, Omaha, Nebraska. All rights reserved. For copies, contact Rod at (816) 525–6339 or www.characterthatcounts.org or Gordon at (308) 293–3891 or www.crosstraining-publishing.com.

Scriptural Blessings to Pray for Your Children

30. Used by permission of the author. Published by NavPress © 2005.

$\mathcal{Jill's}$ ACKNOWLEDGMENTS

$\mathcal{I}$'m grateful for a like-minded coauthor who shares a passion to advocate for kids. Kathy, it's been a joy working with you! Of course, no book is written by one or two people. It's a culmination of years of conversations with friends, family, and other moms in the trenches. With that in mind, I want to express my appreciation to:

Every mom who has shared her story, frustrations, joys, and discoveries with me. Each story has helped formulate the message of this book.

The beautiful people who make up the Hearts at Home leadership team. It is a joy to serve with such a wonderful group of men and women.

My pre-readers who gave valuable initial feedback: Megan, Laury, and Nancy. Your willingness to provide feedback helped make this a better book! Special thanks to Sandra Bishop with MacGregor Literary, who not only offers great feedback but is one of the best literary agents around!

My prayer team: Thank you for standing in the gap for me! Your time on your knees is more important a contribution to this book than any words I write.

The Moody Publishers team: Thank you for believing in the message of this book! We love partnering with you!

Anne, Evan, Erica, Kolya, and Austin: Thank you for allowing me to share your stories. You're the best imperfect kids a mom could ask for! May you embrace the journey of being perfected by God!

Mark: I love you. Thank you for embracing the perfecting process in your life and our marriage—and for filling in the gaps at home while I write!

God: Thank You for Your grace, love, and willingness to use my imperfections for Your purposes!

Kathy's ACKNOWLEDGMENTS

*J*ill, thank you for allowing me the privilege of working with you on this book. I loved watching my ideas come alive as you added your illustrations. Your strategies and mine connected well. We knew they would since we believe the same things about children. God was in this partnership, and I'm grateful and humbled.

I'm also grateful for my extremely talented staff and my dedicated board of directors. These people support and strengthen me. They're multitalented and joyful, and I couldn't do what I do without them. I'm a better person because of them, and my ideas are better, too. Prayer warriors from my church and friends who pray bless me, too.

I'm thankful for the thousands who have heard me speak and reacted to my ideas so I could improve them. I'm honored to be represented by Ambassadors Speakers Bureau and am grateful for their work

. . . .

on my behalf so that Celebrate Kids, Inc., and I can keep influencing thousands of parents, teachers, volunteers, kids, and others.

Of course, without the passion and expertise of people at Moody Publishers, these ideas wouldn't have made it into a book. I'm so grateful for their trust and partnership!

God is amazing, and I'm thrilled that He calls us to be difference-makers for His glory. I'm grateful for His unconditional love and wisdom.

From THE AUTHORS

*D*ear Reader,

We'd love to hear how this book has encouraged you personally! You can find both of us online quite easily!

Jill Savage

Email:	jillannsavage@yahoo.com
Website:	www.HeartsatHome.org
Blog :	www.JillSavage.org
Video:	www.youtube.com/jillannsavage
Facebook:	www.facebook.com/jillsavage.author
	www.facebook.com/heartsathome
Twitter:	@jillsavage @hearts_at_home

Kathy Koch, Ph.D

Email:	nomoreperfect@CelebrateKids.com
Website:	www.CelebrateKids.com
Blog :	www.DrKathyKoch.com
Video:	www.vimeo.com/channels/kathyisms
Facebook:	www.facebook.com/celebratekidsinc
Twitter:	@DrKathyKoch

Make sure you check out *www.NoMorePerfect.com*, where you'll find additional resources to encourage you and to equip you to lead a book study, if you desire.

Joining you in the journey,
Jill and Kathy

HEARTS
at HOME
The Go-To Place for Moms

At Hearts at Home, we know moms—what they're feeling, what questions they have, and the challenges they face. We also believe that moms should know that they're not alone.

That's why we're here.

Hearts at Home exists to provide ongoing education and encouragement in the journey of being a mom.

In addition to this book, we offer a free, monthly eNewsletter called *Hearts On-The-Go* as well as daily encouragement including our Heartbeat Radio Program, our Hearts at Home website, blog, and eCommunity. We've even been known to hang out on Facebook and Twitter for those times when moms need a quick pick-me-up!

Each year, nearly 10,000 moms attend Hearts at Home conferences throughout the United States and abroad. Each event blends powerful keynote sessions with relevant, practical workshops that equip moms to be the best they can be.

No matter what season of motherhood you are navigating, Hearts at Home is here for you. Will you join us?

Hearts at Home
1509 N. Clinton Blvd.
Bloomington, IL 61702
Phone: (309) 828-MOMS
E-mail: hearts@hearts-at-home.org
Web: www.hearts-at-home.org
Facebook: www.facebook.com/heartsathome
Twitter: @hearts_at_home

....

Kathy and the staff and board of Celebrate Kids, Inc., are passionate about helping parents raise the children they were given and not the children they wish they had. We inspire them with hope for tomorrow and solutions that work.

We love equipping, empowering, and encouraging teachers and administrators to better understand their students so they can be more successful. We meet needs by sharing practical and relevant ideas that work, including how to understand tech-savvy kids and keep them engaged.

We help children and teens believe they are created on purpose with purpose with unique gifts and talents. Through Kathy's stories and ideas, they believe in their present value and their future potential. We motivate them to seek solid and true answers to the key questions of life. As a result, they're more content, at peace, and able to strive for excellence.

Since our founding in 1991, all our programs connect in one way or another to our foundational message: People are healthiest when their core needs of security, identity, belonging, purpose, and competence are met in reliable, complete ways.

We influence people through Kathy's presentations in schools, churches, corporations, nonprofit ministries, and conventions. Our webinars, products, email newsletter, Facebook page, blog, and Vimeo videos are all designed to provide hope and practical solutions that work.

Your *No More Perfect* journey continues online.

Embracing imperfection is tough, isn't it? Whether it's with ourselves, our kids, our spouse or just life in general, it's hard to let the world know that we just don't have it all together.

That's why we've created a website to be a road map for your *No More Perfect* journey. It's a community where you'll find encouragement, connection with other moms and a space where you can just be yourself!

Join us at **www.NoMorePerfect.com** for additional resources (including ways to share information about the books with your friends and materials to use with moms groups or book clubs) and ongoing conversations (you can even share your story!) that will help you let go of imperfect and embrace authentic!

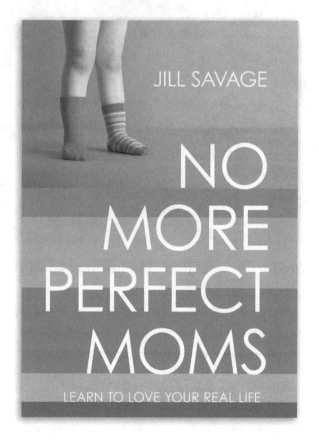

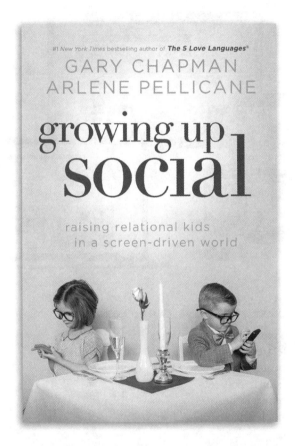

THE 5 LOVE LANGUAGES OF CHILDREN

Not only will Dr. Gary Chapman and Dr. Ross Campbell help you discover your child's love language, but you'll also learn how the love languages can help you discipline more effectively, build a foundation of unconditional love for your child, and understand the link between successful learning and the love languages.

REAL MOMS... REAL JESUS

What does Jesus know about the peanut-butter-and-jelly life of a mom? Plenty! Jill Savage brings lessons from the life of Jesus right down to the laundry-filled, sticky-fingered days every mother knows. In *Real Moms...Real Jesus*, Savage continually reminds the reader that Jesus is not an unattainable deity, but a Friend who understands.

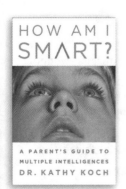

HOW AM I SMART?

When parents determine ways children can be smart, they'll better understand their own children's educational needs and how they learn best. This must-read book by Dr. Kathy Koch reveals roots of behavior struggles and relationship conflicts, and their possible solutions. Dr. Kathy unfolds the eight different ways intelligence manifests itself through the "multiple intelligences."

A PERFECT PET FOR PEYTON

Gary Chapman and Rick Osborne help children (ages 5–12) learn about the importance of love in this wonderfully imaginative and classically illustrated children's hardcover book featuring four-color illustrations (with hidden details!) by Wilson Williams, Jr., based on Gary's bestselling *The 5 Love Languages*®.